For Christopher

with all good wishes

Vasant Yayon

May 23/2009

LOVE
and
SAND

An RAF Flyer's memoir of love, lies and military
mayhem in the
World War II
Deserts of North Africa

Howard M. Layton

Published by: Three Spires Publishing
Post Office Box 5267
Brookfield, CT 06804-5267 U.S.A.

Printed in the United States of America

Library of Congress Catalog Card Number 2007904839

Layton, Howard M.

Love and Sand

An RAF Flyer's memoir of love, lies and military
mayhem in the World War II
Deserts of North Africa

Howard M. Layton

Interior design by Barbara Hudson, Data Entry Services
Cover Model: Corinne Ferry

First EditionISBN 978-0-9676008-5-7

For Nárcissza,

who knows about selflessness and sacrifice.

Three Spires Publishing
Post Office Box 5267
Brookfield, CT 06804-5267 U.S.A.

HISTORICAL ACCURACY

Departure from the strict truth occurs in two places in this memoir, one military and one non-military. In chapter five, the brawl is a little exaggerated to emphasize and summarize the author's immaturity and quarrelsome nature at the time, and in chapter sixteen, the account of the mishap suffered by the author and his fellow flyers on the Trans-Africa aircraft delivery flight, is exaggerated to reflect harrowing experiences reported by crews of previous missions. We were indeed lost for a while (through the Author's own ineptitude), but we all eventually made it to the El Geneina airfield without running out of fuel.

Note also that although the submarine rescue episode referred to in chapter eight is confirmed in naval records and in the book 'The Winston Specials' by Archie Munro, the precise <u>location</u> that I have ascribed to that rescue may or may not be accurate. The author's memory about exactly where this occurred is hazy, and the above book does not specify the location of the rescue or the name of the submarine involved. For this reason, the name given herein to the submarine, is fictitious—and intentionally improbable. (See also the following acknowledgement list).

Aside from the exceptions itemized above, this account is as accurate as the author's own records and memory, and the extensive and detailed archives at Kew Gardens and other British museums and literature, have been able to make it.

❖ ❖ ❖

Note for researchers: Readers interested in learning more about the military events listed below, and described at length in these pages, should note that detailed information is available in 'Operations Record Books,' Air 27\1198 and Air 27\1375 at the British National Archives at Kew Gardens, Surrey:

The Raid on the Italian bases in Abyssinia.
The RAF escort of the convoys in the Red Sea and during the evacuation of Greece.
The RAF close-support bombing raids at El Alamein.
Our public-relations activities in Tripolitania.
The Trans-Africa aircraft delivery route. (See also "Pan Africa – Across the Sahara in 1941 with Pan Am." (Paladwr Press), referenced elsewhere in this account.

Acknowledgments

The events described in this narrative occurred more than sixty years ago, so the writer found it necessary to seek a good deal of help in refreshing his memory about important times and dates relating to the happenings of that tumultuous era, and also to re-learn a great deal of technical information about the aircraft in which he flew, and those he encountered. Fortunately, comprehensive and accurate archives relative to every facet of World War II do exist, and the following is a list of those the author found most helpful:

Mr. Andy Simpson
Royal Air Force Museum
Graham Park Way
London NW9 5 LL, UK

Mrs. R Ahmed and Mr. A J Williams
Public Records Office
The National Archives
Kew, Richmond,
Surrey TW9 4DU, UK

John (Smudge) Smith, (An institution in himself).
Aircraft Restoration Company, Duxford, UK

Reader information Services Department
Public Record Office

The National Archives
Kew, Richmond, Surrey TW9 4DU, UK

PMA Sec IM1B, Room 5, Building 248A

RAF Innsworth, Gloucester, GL3 1EZ, UK

Air Historical Branch (RAF)
Building 266, RAF Bentley Priory
Stanmore
Middlesex, HA7 3HH, UK

I also thank Dr. Somogyi Balázs, Bertha Divine, Lisa
Wright Jenkins, and Ann Sheinhouse, for their valuable
suggestions on reviewing the manuscript.

For their skillful contributions to the layout of the
dust jacket, I thank Liviu Marian and Tucsi Cseh.

My thanks go also to Tom Culbert and Andy
Dawson, Authors of "Pan Africa – Across the Sahara in
1941 with Pan Am." (Paladwr Press). Their book
presents a fine example of Anglo-American cooperation
in the rapid up-grading of the Trans-Africa aircraft
delivery route, which served the allies so effectively in
the build-up of fighter power for the El Alamein conflict.

I thank my editor, Theodore A. Rees Cheney, whose
patience and humor have provided me with much
entertainment as well as meticulous guidance and editing
of my writing.

I thank Brian Knight for permission to use his
striking portrait of the Blenheim IV aircraft (see photo
at rear).

I thank British archivist George Malcolmson, RN Submarine Museum, for his most tenacious researching of the submarine incident described herein, and I thank Bill Keeny of the US Submarine Learning Center, Public Affairs, and Keith Humpleby of the British HQDNRHQ for leading me to George.

I thank the members of the Rollingwood Book Club, Brookfield, CT for their revue of the manuscript and for their constructive suggestions.

Finally, I thank my three daughters, Christine, Alison and Paulette, whose comprehensive reviews and suggestions made 'Love and Sand' a better book.

GLOSSARY OF TECHNICAL, FOREIGN AND UNUSUAL TERMS

Ambrose Orchestra: A leading English dance band of the time.

Aywa Effendi: Arabic for 'Yes sir'.

Black Balls: Large metal globes hoisted to the tops of tall masts at Egyptian beaches when powerful currents made swimming dangerous.

Blenheim IV: A light twin-engined Bomber built at the Filton works of the Bristol Aircraft Company, and elsewhere in Britain. Used extensively as a fighter as well, and notable for its suitability for use in most environments. A Canadian version, known as the 'Bolingbroke' was intended to supplement the production of the English factories, but in practice, was used only for service within Canada and the United States, largely for training purposes.

BSA Spider 350: A popular British motor cycle made by the Birmingham Small Arms Company.

Bukkra fi mish mish: An Arabic expression for which the literal translation is 'Tomorrow, when the apricots bloom.' Note, however, that apricots do not bloom.

Bwana: Swahili for Sir or Master.

Chatti: An earthenware jug for water or wine.

Chocks: Wedge-shaped wooden blocks placed at the front of an aircraft's main wheels to prevent inadvertent movement when throttles are opened for the engine run-up routine.

Crikey: A British North Country expletive.

CR 42: An Italian biplane fighter aircraft of between wars vintage, typically equipped with guns that fired shells of about 0.4 inch caliber.

Fûl: A sandwich consisting of a pita bread pocket filled with a hot mixture of fava beans and other vegetables. As popular with Arabs as pizza is for Italians, and hamburger for Americans. Retail 'Fûl' stores abounded like English fish and chip shops because of their

appeal to all classes of the
population.

Galabia: A loose, ankle-length garment,
usually white or light-colored, worn
by both men and women.

Gills: Ventilator slats hinged in a
continuous array around the
cowling or 'casing' of an aircraft's
radial engine to permit free airflow
for engine cooling purposes when
opened for ground run-up, and an
aerodynamically smooth contour
when closed for flight.

Henry Hall
Orchestra: The official BBC dance-band of the
day.

Hornet: A popular English Wolseley sports
car of the times.

Houseboat: As its name implies, a barge with
the equivalent of a house built into
it. Such craft were designed for
navigating canals and rivers rather
than the open seas.

In-line astern: The term used in the RAF to
describe the arrangement whereby
aircraft would follow the leader in a
single nose-to-tail line.

Jumbo: Swahili term for 'Greetings.' or
                        'How are you.'

Junkers JU88:   A very capable German medium
                        bomber of between wars vintage
                        used extensively in both the
                        European and Middle-Eastern
                        theatres of World War II.

Khamsin: Pronounced 'Khamseen.' A desert
                        wind, often powerful and
                        persistent, causing blinding
                        sandstorms and making travel
                        virtually impossible.

Laban zi bahdi: A popular middle-eastern appetizer
                        of sour cream (Crème renversé),
                        mint, chopped cucumber and ice.
                        Origin not clear, probably Syrian;
                        note that 'Laban' is the Arabic
                        word for yogurt.

Massai: The name of a tribe of African
                        warriors noted for their bravery.

Mousaka: A baked dish of Greek origin using
                        rice, minced lamb, chopped
                        vegetables and spices. Popular
                        throughout middle-eastern
                        countries.

NDB: Non-Directional Beacon. A
                        powerful omni-directional radio
                        transmitter, sending an identifying
                        three letter call-sign in all

directions. Serves even today, as a valuable navigation aid.

Pukka gen:
An RAF expression meaning 'the true story' or 'the most reliable' information. 'Gen,' widely used alone in RAF slang in place of 'information.'

Stella:
The brand name of an Egyptian brewed beer.

Strafing:
A term used to describe an aerial attack on a ground target, using machine guns commonly mounted in the nose or wings of the attacking aircraft, and fixed in position so that the aircraft itself has to be aimed at the target.

Track:
The distance between the left and right wheels of an automobile. The length of the axle. The narrow-tracked 'Wolseley Hornet' was especially prone to turn over when driven at speed around bends.

Tonneau cover:
A protective encasement for storing the retracted soft-top of a Convertible automobile.

Vauxhall:
The brand name of a popular British automobile.

Wizard: RAF slang word meaning 'fine' or
               'excellent' or 'admirable.'

FOREWORD

This book is about the years in a man's life when nothing is impossible, when the sky is the limit and all can be conquered. Howard Layton remembers every minute of those early years of his life and conveys not only their events, but also the sounds, smells, panic and jubilation that accompanied them, setting down his story in eloquent and smoothly flowing language so that it feels you are there.

The early years of World War II is the time, and the skies of North Africa the setting for this memoir of an English air-force officer, whose assignment was to fight the forces of Rommel on that hot and sandy continent. For him, those bombs defended his homeland, defended freedom and democracy.

Besides being about war, this book is also about love. It is about meeting beautiful women but never forgetting that one, that special one. It is also about a young man searching for direction, figuring out who he is and what he wants to do with his life. It is about a state of mind when nothing yet is off limits, when one can select the continent one wants to live on, the religion one wants to practice, in a time when anything and everything is possible.

Béla G. Lipták

Author's Note:

Béla Lipták is an Adjunct Professor of Yale University, Fellow of the Instrument Society of America and recipient of the Life Achievement Award for his teachings, writings and inventions.

Among the many books he has written, his memoir: 'A Testament of Revolution,' describes his own desperate and heroic struggle for freedom as one of the leading participants in the Hungarian Revolution.

INTRODUCTION

There I was, sitting on the roof of the General Electric Company works in the suburb of Stoke, Coventry, muttering to myself as I wielded a ten-inch brush, slapping camouflage paint over as much of the extensive asphalt surface as I could reach. It wasn't at all clear to me why they were paying me to do this job, while I should have been down below on the production line, inspecting radio-set wiring and looking for badly soldered joints. But since I was not privy to the high level decisions that had, I assumed, led to my present activity, I went on dipping and slapping. In a while, as my tanned, sandy-haired pal, Doug Philips climbed the ladder and handed me a mug of hot, sweet tea, I took a break to bask in the warmth of that sunny October afternoon.

I had other things to worry about. I was nineteen years old and madly in love, trying desperately to do something about my quick temper and the jealous behavior that Verna, the girl of my dreams, described as immature and 'hopeless.' I had to do something about that, she said, or she would give up on me.

Unthinkable. I just couldn't let it happen.

In any case, I couldn't understand why this painting fever was necessary at all, or why all those pessimists were going on about war, when all the mayhem was so far away across countless miles of sea, so remote from our island fortress. Besides, hadn't that Chamberlain chap made a deal with the Nazis, and hadn't everything been settled so that we would have 'peace in our time'?

I sipped my tea and considered the possibilities. What if there really were a showdown and we had to get involved? What if we really had to fight those buggers? Wouldn't that be something! Doug and I would join the RAF, of course, and we would become pilots and bomb the daylights out of all those strutting Nazis.

Man, what a showdown that would be!

I almost wished it would happen.

Passport photo of the author, taken at
Heliopolis, Cairo. 1944

ONE

Aden in the Indian Ocean

Early 1941

The port engine was on fire and nobody knew. Unaware of that developing crisis, I looked across at the captain's face to see how he was faring. Squadron Leader James Pike, not yet thirty years old and already a veteran of many bombing and strafing sorties, was preoccupied with his flight instruments. Small beads of sweat glistened on his brow and along the length of his aristocratic nose. The set of his jaw and the creases around his eyes revealed some strain and fatigue, but his calm demeanor had not changed. With eyes focused on the airspeed indicator and altimeter, he was attending to his primary responsibility—flying the airplane. Never mind the holes in the wings, the smell of fuel and burning oil, or the intermittent grating sound from the starboard engine. Fly the airplane. We clawed our way up the last few hundred feet toward the mountain ridge ahead.

Despite the engine noise, our Blenheim IV was in other respects relatively quiet now. The staccato crack of

1

cannon shells boring into our wings and fuselage, and the sharp thudding against the armor plate behind us, had ceased. The CR42 biplanes, having waited high above us to dive on our tail as we returned for our second attack on this Italian occupied Abyssinian airfield, had eventually lost their advantage. Unable to match even our own modest speed, they'd turned away—but not before they'd done a good deal of damage.

Still in shock, it wasn't until the captain had barked his instructions for the second time that I snapped out of my daze and became conscious again of my surroundings.

"Check on the air gunner! See if he's OK." .

Yes, of course, better check on our stoic air-gunner. Shaking my head, I forced myself into action. Squeezing through the cramped space between the seats, I crawled back along the fuselage through acrid smoke and the odor of burning oil, rubber, grease and plastic and tapped him on his lean, muscular thigh.

"How is it, Geordie?" I yelled.

I heard his muffled reply that he was just fine.

"Anything bleeding or broken?"

"No, no complaints."

After a quick glance around to assess the extent of damage to the rear fuselage area, I noted particularly that the radio equipment stack had been blown apart. I made my way back again to my navigator's seat and leaned across toward the captain.

"He's OK sir, but the radio equipment has taken a hit."

Pike responded with a curt nod.

Something distracted me as I glanced at him again—
something out there, past the front of his flying helmet
and through the port window. The portside Mercury
radial engine and its three-bladed prop seemed to be
doing just fine. But what was that? A wisp of smoke
coming from the propeller hub? I stared, fascinated.
Nothing. I must have imagined it. I turned back to the
business of checking our course, and thinking about the
fact that this was, after all, what we had come for— to
take the war to the enemy even all these thousands of
miles from our homeland. Yes indeed, we'd been having
it too easy.

Only yesterday morning, my buddy and mentor, Eric
(Crut) Cruttenden, tall and swashbuckling, had walked
into our barracks hut with a broad smile on his tanned
aristocratic face. He'd just taken a stroll over to the mess
to see whether there'd been any last minute additions to
the operations board. There'd been none, so tomorrow we
would stand down. We would rest, read, play soccer, or
swim. We'd have the day to ourselves. Crut made his
way down the long dormitory and parked himself in the
chair next to his bed, just across from mine. He tipped
his head back in his characteristic manner and regarded
me with his lively blue eyes. "So what are we up to
tomorrow, Turner, soccer or swimming?" Turner was my
nick-name, on account of the fact that Turner Leighton
was one of the popular singers of the day.

I wasn't a keen soccer player, and even if I had been,
I wouldn't have enjoyed rushing around in the burning
heat of the Aden climate. That, as far as I was concerned,
was for all those other lunatics who seemed to have

become acclimated. Practically every chance they had, they would be out there, banging that ball around.

"I think a day on the beach will suit me fine, Crut. What about you?"

He flashed all those white teeth again. "Good, let's do it."

The beach, less than a quarter mile from our corrugated iron, pre-fabricated Nissen huts, had long stretches of fine sand for sunbathing and innumerable caves and rock formations to explore, but because of the shark hazard, swimming in the waters of the bay had been strictly forbidden. The top brass in Cairo had made it very clear that they did not expect to train good men and transport them all the way to some remote corner of the Middle Eastern Desert, to have them eaten up by sharks. To court such risks, they said, was not at all in the interest of the war effort, and they would not tolerate it. On the other hand, young, fit, and able-bodied servicemen needed exercise and a good way to keep cool during the heat of the day. It was too much to expect them to watch those foaming white breakers pounding the beach so close at hand and not yearn to plunge in just now and then.

The local administration had solved the problem by building a huge swimming pool, complete with a three-tiered diving board, right on the beach. It was a success from the moment it opened, and even the most ardent of the swimmers found it adequate for their needs. We spent a great deal of our off-duty time throwing ourselves off those boards, belly flopping or diving

4

cleanly according to our capabilities. Some of us wore swimming trunks, but because there were no members of the fair sex among us, most enjoyed the freedom and incomparable sensuality of swimming through the lukewarm velvet unhampered by clothing of any sort.

Gradually, the early redness of our skins turned to light tan, then to darker shades, and finally, on certain parts of our bodies, almost to black. For reasons that we were not able to fathom, the deepest tanning occurred on and around our genital areas, and by the time we were all fully accustomed to the effects of the sun on various parts of our bodies, we were placing bets on whose penis and testicles would eventually become the blackest. Those of us who lived long enough would eventually pay a high price for our indifference to the potent ultraviolet radiation to which we exposed ourselves with such abandon under the Yemen sun. The melanoma that developed on my own chest thirty years later was attributed to the long-term effects of those times when we lived as if there were no tomorrow. For many of us, of course, that's the way it was.

Many weeks passed before letters from home reached us in the RAF desert stations, and as I learned later, some two months had passed before our first letters had reached our loved ones. The letters and parcels from home were life-lines to all of us; constant reminders that the people and the things that mattered to us were still there waiting for our eventual return, and that if we were lucky enough to last the course, there would be a some-day when we would be able to pick up our lives again where we'd left off. There would be a future, and the letters helped us preserve our faith in that future, helped us to hope.

Evidently, Elaine and Fred Stemmet, the big-hearted couple whom my friend Johnny and I had met in the course of our refueling stop at Cape Town on the way out, were aware, too, of the significance of these lifelines. Without fail, every month since we'd left Cape Town, Elaine had sent Johnny and me substantial parcels of eatables and wearables and a similar number of letters. The parcels and letters had not always arrived as regularly as Elaine had sent them, for we'd been moving around in difficult-to-reach corners of middle-eastern territory, but I was able to tell from the postmarks that the mailing of those letters and parcels was, for her, an unfailing monthly ritual. I was lucky. I was never short of communication with the outside world for very long; never short of the knowledge that someone cared about how I was faring. Between my family and my fiancée Verna, and Elaine, I was constantly reminded that there were people who wanted to know that I was well, cheerful, and coping; that the socks and underwear they'd sent, were the right kind for the climate and that the jars of preserved fruit and cans of Spam, and McConaghie's Meat and Vegetables, were what I liked. Yes, I was lucky; too lucky.

Notice to standby for a strafing mission had appeared on the notice-board late in the afternoon, so as things turned out, we didn't get to go swimming after all.

We'd taken off at 10.30 hours from our base at Khormaksar near Aden on the southeastern tip of the

6

Yemen Territory. Since our bunch had arrived four months previously, assignments for 203 Squadron had been confined to escorting convoys up and down the Red Sea, or carrying out other patrol missions. Mostly, we flew at around seventeen thousand feet, ready to dive on any enemy aircraft that might come near. Routine work and pretty dull. A few enterprising intruders occasionally appeared in the distance, but were quick to retreat when they caught sight of the escort planes. Today however, our orders had been quite different. Intelligence had determined that the airfield at Makale, in Abbysinia, was undergoing expansion and rapidly enlarging its fleet of military aircraft based there. 203 Squadron had received orders to carry out a strafing attack on that airfield, using pairs of Blenheim IVF aircraft which, aside from the two Browning guns in the upper turret, carried four forward-firing Brownings under the nose and another one in the port wing.

A reconnaissance flight had checked out the target area the previous day, and the aerial photos showed substantial concentrations of airplanes sitting on the ramps outside the hangars (Map 1). Those were the clusters we were ordered to destroy. The raids were to be accomplished with the use of incendiary ammunition, the idea being to dive on the airfield and set fire to as many parked aircraft as possible. Using ammunition that left visible traces of its trajectory, it would be possible to see that the incendiaries were finding their mark, and if not, the aircraft's flight path could be immediately corrected to ensure a direct hit on the target.

We also had a tactical advantage, for the airfield was located in a valley just beyond the western slopes of a mountain range. If we made a low approach through the mountain pass to the south of the field, our engines would not be heard until we were almost upon our targets. By the time the Italians realized they were being attacked, it would already be over.

We would come in low across the treetops so that anti-aircraft batteries would not have time to get a bead on us. Then, within a mile of the target area, we would gain a little altitude, just enough to get into position for the shallow dive into the swarm of parked aircraft, and with enough ground clearance left to pull up and away when we'd finished the job.

The defending Italian CR42 aircraft would be no problem either. True, they were incredibly maneuverable, and each packed a wicked half-inch canon in its nose. But a biplane of between-wars vintage was simply not fast enough to catch a Blenheim IV. We'd be in and out before they got off the ground. And that's exactly how it went—in the beginning.

At the morning briefing we'd arranged that the two Blenheims would fly out from Khormaksar together. Then, to avoid getting in each other's way, our number two would fall a half-mile behind as we reached the mountain pass. Our own aircraft would go in first and pick a primary target area, and number two, coming up behind, would attack the next thickest cluster of airplanes in its path.

We approached the pass at 12.35 hrs and our number two dropped behind as planned. We made our way around the southern slopes, staying low, close to the hillside. In minutes we emerged on the western side. Then we saw it through the haze— the Makale airfield nestled in the valley to the northwest. There appeared to be little flying activity in progress and we were unable to detect any anti-aircraft action. We flew down the western slope into the valley, Pike still hugging the treetops and now maneuvering into position for the best direction of approach. The closely packed swarm of enemy aircraft included transports, reconnaissance planes, CR 42s and trainers, all parked on a paved ramp at the eastern entrance of a pair of large hangars. Pike flew west until we were aligned immediately to the south of the ramp, from which approach he would be able to pump incendiaries into the maximum number of aircraft without having to contend with a departure over the tops of the hangars. As he then banked to the north, the enemy barrage began. Thick black puffs appeared at our port side and directly ahead, but they were all too high to be harmful. Our briefing had been accurate; they would have difficulty hitting us until we were on our way out after the raid. Then we'd have to watch out.

Pike didn't have to climb again to achieve an optimum angle of attack. The contours of the valley were such that from our present position, we could stay down low, close to the trees, right on up to the perimeter of the airport and still preserve a shallow but optimum dive angle in relation to the target ahead.

In less than a minute we were there, our tracer incendiaries illuminating their flight paths as they bored their way into the engines, wings and fuselages of aircraft of all types and sizes. People in uniform ran in all directions; fighter pilots rushed out to their biplanes to give chase. Others were already taking off.

As Pike pulled up and away, an explosion just behind us rocked our plane.

Geordie, yelling over the intercom, sounded as excited as a small boy at a fireworks display. "Oh boy, what a sight for sore eyes; there's fire all over the place. It's spreadin' through the bloody lot! It's settin' fire to the hangars. Oh man, what a picnic. Number two's in there now, ploughin' into them transports on the side. One of 'em's burnin' like a bonfire."

I breathed deeply and loosened my collar.

It was over. The smoke and wreckage were left behind as we intercepted the road snaking its way north along the base of the valley. Following the plan we'd worked out at our morning briefing, we'd stay low and fly up the valley road, attacking any military traffic we might encounter along the way. Then, once out of range of the airfield's anti-aircraft defenses, we'd turn east, climb back up the mountain range and head for home.

A sound plan, but James Pike had other ideas. He'd noted that the pass through which we'd flown to make our approach from the south, was matched by another convenient pass not far beyond the northern perimeter of the airfield, and we were already approaching it. As soon as we were abreast of it, he banked to the right and headed straight up the slopes toward the opening. Once over the crest, he banked right again, following the slopes around to the south. I realized then what he planned—to go around for a second attack—and that certainly wasn't part of our briefing.

A surprise attack was one thing, but a return for a second run was to my mind, close to suicidal. My stomach churned.

I pressed my mike button and was about to speak— to remind the captain that those CR42s would now be waiting for us with plenty of altitude so they could dive on us, but as soon as the thought occurred to me I saw its futility. He knew the facts at least as well as I. There was nothing useful for me to say. Squadron Leader Pike was not being rash or foolhardy. He was not that kind of officer. He'd simply decided to use his authority as flight commander to take advantage of an opportunity to inflict considerably more damage on the enemy. He'd decided that the increased danger to our aircraft and its crew was a risk worth taking.

The station commander's quiet and intense words at the morning briefing came back to me:

"You can do your duty, or you can do more than your duty. The difference, gentlemen, is victory."

"Well," I muttered to myself, "we're about to do more than our duty. No doubt about that, old bean. So it had better be worth it. We'd better flatten the sods."

We approached from almost the same southerly vantage point that had served us barely twenty minutes previously. Pike aimed our aircraft at two fuel trucks parked near a cluster of training planes. He began firing at fairly long range, correcting his angle of approach as our tracer bullets revealed their flight path. The nearest truck burst into flames immediately. We were almost upon it. With only split-seconds to spare, Pike climbed steeply away to the right. At 400 feet, he leveled out and followed the road north along the valley floor. Then, as soon as we were clear of the target area he brought the aircraft down near tree-top level again.

Geordie's voice came over the intercom from the turret again, his words tumbling out so fast it was difficult to decipher them.

"Bloody inferno— oh, oh, look at that—hangars as well! Everythin's goin' up! Oh crikey just look at that!"

More targets ahead. Military convoys driving north. Pike lowered the nose again and pumped incendiaries into a line of trucks as we closed in on them. Soldiers fell over each other and dived for cover as the transports disgorged their human load. Then, just as quickly, we'd left them behind and were climbing the slopes as we changed course toward the east.

But this time the Italians were ready for us. The small CR42 biplanes that we'd seen taking off as we'd made our first attack, had now had time to climb to several thousand feet in preparation for a possible second attack. They were waiting for us, circling over the airfield as we approached for our second round. Diving on us from their patrol positions, they were able to achieve a high enough airspeed to stay on our tail for many fateful moments as we turned onto our easterly departure course. The odds had shifted.

Geordie yelled. "Captain, we've got company! There are two of 'em on our tail. Oh bloody hell . . ."

The sharp clatter of shells striking our wings and fuselage interrupted him, merging with the noise and staccato chatter of his two Browning guns as he returned their fire. Pike banked the aircraft left, then right, in an attempt to shake off our pursuers as we climbed. Several more sickening thuds on the armor plate, followed. Then Geordie's voice again.

"Hey, I think I winged one. They're droppin' back, chief—Lord bless us, they can't keep up. Crikey, I did it! My bird's gone down in flames. The smoke . . ."

The headphones went dead. The familiar background hiss disappeared.

We continued our climb up the slopes.

Pike leaned across and yelled above the engine noise. "Where's number two?"

"I don't know. I'll go back and check with Geordie."

I worked my way back to Geordie's turret. I tapped him on the thigh and he bent down and put his mouth to my ear.

"What's up Turner?"

"What happened to number two?"

"When we turned right up the hillside, he continued on up the road. I don't think he saw us turn off, so he stayed with the original plan. He probably thought he'd catch up with us."

"You okay?"

"Sure. 'specially since I knocked that bugger out of the sky."

"Congratulations." I banged him on his thigh and worked my way back to my seat. Leaning across to Pike, I yelled, "Number two went home. Geordie reckons he didn't see us turn off and assumed we were up ahead of him."

I turned back to my charts to check what our position would be when we topped the ridge. Better make it a direct course from here on. Allowing for the prevailing wind, that would be about 110° magnetic. I drew the new course-line on the chart and began to work out our probable ETA at our Aden base. We would cross the ridge at about 13.20 hrs. Given the moderate westerly wind that had prevailed most of the day, we would expect to touch down back at base around 1530 hrs. I turned to the captain to check on our remaining fuel, and as I did so, my eyes were drawn again, past the front of his head and through the left window to the port engine beyond. There it was—a thin wisp of smoke, wrapping itself tightly around the hub of the propeller assembly.

No mistaking it this time. It was there. It thickened as I watched, coiling itself around the hub, dividing itself into skeins that wound themselves around the roots of the propeller blades.

With unblinking eyes still locked onto the steadily growing knots of smoke, and forgetting that the intercom was dead, I pressed my mike button instinctively. Nothing. I reached out and tapped the captain's shoulder. He turned his face toward me briefly, acknowledging with a nod that he'd seen what I had seen. Then, with a faint smile, he busied himself again with his controls and his instruments.

Was that a smile of resignation, or was it a brave man's reaction to dire circumstances—an attempt to gird himself for the trials ahead, and perhaps reassure me too? I just couldn't tell. I wiped my brow and tried to get back to my charts.

Several minutes passed, the engines beating out their slightly whining drone as we climbed. Then it happened. As I continued to watch the now dense mantle of smoke belching from the port engine cowling, the entire three-bladed propeller assembly, still turning at speed, detached itself from the airplane and moved smoothly forward into space. For three or four mesmerizing seconds, still spinning, it held its position about three feet directly ahead of the engine shaft that it had just left. Then, as I continued to stare in disbelief, it fell away.

The ridge ahead loomed large and wide. We had only one engine now, to get us over the top, and even that one, we now realized, was not operating on all cylinders. There was nowhere to go but down—hopefully under control and still flying, but down just the same. For a brief moment, the airplane skidded to the left and crabbed its way across the forest below. Then, as the captain put his weight on the right rudder and reached for the horizontal trim, we straightened out again. He was aiming for a small break in the line of trees at the summit just ahead, but it was already clear to me that we were losing altitude a bit too fast to clear them. I can only assume that, at the last minute, a heaven-sent updraft of the kind that glider pilots pray for had arrived just in time to lift us over the top. At any rate, if we were destined to lose our lives on some foreign soil, it evidently was not going to happen here on top of these remote Abbysinian mountains. We skimmed over the treetops, clearing them by not more than thirty feet. Then quite quickly, the terrain fell away ahead of us, and the way was clear.

A vast panorama of fields, forest, scrub and desert spread out across our flight path as we left the ridge behind. The smoke in the cockpit and fuselage gradually dissipated. Time to take stock of our situation. We were going down, no doubt about that, but it would be a gradual descent. As I checked the airspeed indicator, and our altitude loss per minute, my rough calculations showed that with any luck we would probably make it to the coast. We'd ditch about a quarter of the way across the Red Sea. That is, of course, if we weren't leaking fuel.

The Squadron Leader's voice came over the intercom. "Give me a new course. I want the shortest route directly to the coast."

I wrestled with my charts and issued a correction to 085°. We'd cross the shoreline near the small township of Edd. From there, we'd make our way over toward the Eastern Shore. If my calculations were off, and by some miracle we managed to reach the other side, we would make an off-airport landing on the eastern shore, where there would be some chance of friendly forces finding us.

The acrid odors of burned rubber and plastic faded and merged with the smell of our own sweat. The captain trimmed the aircraft to a carefully calculated rate of descent to maximize distance traveled for every hundred feet of altitude lost.

And so, with occasional course corrections for wind-shift as we left the mountain range behind, our flight became relatively smooth and controlled once more. We flew on, slowly losing altitude as the miles and the minutes passed. By the time we could see the coastline ahead, our altimeter reading put us at less than 2500 feet above the now gently undulating coastal terrain.

The choice now, was to crash land on the beach this side, probably to be picked up by the enemy or nomads from the hills, or force on and ditch somewhere out there in the green and hungry sea; a difficult choice indeed. We'd been told at our flight briefing that the nomads around the coastal areas were primitive and bloodthirsty, and we'd learned enough from airmen who had crashed in these territories before and somehow made their way back, that our chances of avoiding an exceedingly painful death on this side of the water, were not promising.

On the other hand, ditching in the shark-infested waters of the Red Sea was not an attractive prospect either. Our radio communication gear had been the first casualty of our encounter with the CR42s. The main transceiver had taken a direct hit and had literally split apart.

The captain made his decision. "Aden will be looking for us once we've passed our ETA, so we'll get as far out as we can, and hope that some friendly chaps will spot us and pick us up."

As we left the coastline behind us, the altimeter showed us at 1200ft and descending. I turned my attention to the matter of survival at sea. Then the order came.

"Check the dinghy and the inflation gear—and see that the flares are OK."

"Yes sir!"

I climbed to the back and passed the message on to Geordie. I waited while he struggled out of his gun cupola and shuffled around to the life raft storage area. After what seemed an eternity I heard his voice again.

"There's no dinghy. We didn't bring one."

Pike just nodded when I gave him the news. He seemed to have expected it. But he didn't change course to head back to the shore as I'd expected.

We just flew on, peering through the windshield as, minute by minute, the roiling sea reached up to meet us.

TWO

W as that it, then? Had Pike chosen to die at sea rather than die at the hands of the coastal nomads? Or was he putting his faith in some plan that I was not privy to? Could he not see that we would have a far better hope of survival if we opted for the beach behind us and took our chances with the natives, rather than continue on our present course toward certain death by drowning—or by being eaten by sharks?

I sat there struggling between my natural reluctance to question my chief's decision and my growing conviction that if I didn't say something pretty soon, I would burst.

I leaned across and tapped him on the shoulder. As he turned his head, he must have seen the question in my eyes. Before I could speak, he pointed to the emergency boost control on the upper right corner of the instrument panel. He tapped it several times and moved his hand up and down in front of the control knob in a motion indicative of turning it on and off. I nodded that I understood and was immediately relieved to know that he had some plan in mind that might give us some chance of survival. The fact that his plan was, to my mind, akin to asking for a miracle, did not matter. However slim the chances of it working, it seemed to me to have the edge on the alternatives.

The Blenheim IV airplane emergency power control, known as 'Plus 9 Boost,' permits the pilot to race an engine beyond its normal operating limits for a very brief period. This was the aircraft's last-resort ace-in-the-hole resource. In dire circumstances, the pilot could reach up and grab the Plus-9 handle, pull it hard, breaking the retaining wire that prevented accidental usage. Pulled out to its horizontal position, it boosted engine power from its normal maximum of plus 6 to plus 9 boost. It could be applied for up to one minute. Beyond that time limit, rapid overheating would, according to the aircraft's handbook, destroy the engine.

It had certainly not occurred to me that this extreme power level could be used for more than a one-shot effort at survival, but Pike, already convinced that the emergency boost would be sufficient to stop our descent, had other ideas. But what chance was there that at this extreme performance level the engine would last for more than a couple of minutes?

I was not about to comment on that. As a sergeant crew member on his first really dangerous mission, there was no way I could say anything useful. The captain, an experienced and highly skilled airman, knew what he was doing.

At 500 feet above the water, Pike grasped the boost handle and wrenched it forward and down, fracturing the retaining wire. The engine noise and vibration increased immediately, and the pitch of the whining rose several notches, but there was no immediate change in the rate of our descent. The waiting seemed interminable.

The altimeter reading continued to fall, but at about 350 feet above sea level, the increased engine power began to have an effect. The needle hovered there as our loss of altitude was arrested. Then, slowly, oh so slowly, we began to gain altitude again. But engine temperature was rising, too. In less than a minute, the needle had reached the red line. We had barely reached 500 feet.

Pike turned off the boost. We began a slow descent again, and within seconds, engine temperature began to ease back down. But not fast enough. The needle was still showing some elevation of temperature when the altimeter registered 200 feet. We had to climb again. Pike re-applied the boost. The descent stopped and we began to climb, but now the engine temperature rose more quickly and stayed above the red line, remaining in that condition even after Pike again turned off the boost and we were on our way down once more.

I felt the dryness in my mouth. We weren't going to make it; that much was evident. There was no way this damaged and overheated mass of machinery could last more than one or two more minutes, and at our present single-engine airspeed, we were still a good forty minutes away from the eastern shore.

Strangely, as this realization came to me—that we were going to die—the cold fear that had been building inside me gradually subsided. I became conscious only of a deep sadness for all that might have been; for the loss of any opportunity to eventually see my home again, to

21

pick up where I'd left off; to be with my family once more. I would not be taking that boat when it was all over. There would be no reunion with my mother and my brother, and there would be no opportunity for me to atone for the hurt I'd inflicted on Verna, my wonderful girl back home—for the emotional damage I'd caused her, and for the unforgivable lie I'd told her. There would be no chance now to plan for that longed-for day when I could be by her side again, confessing the lie that had haunted me for so long, and begging for her forgiveness.

If I'd been a believer in a compassionate god, I would have prayed fervently right then for a miracle that would somehow keep us aloft 'til we reached the Yemen coast. But I knew that if there were any way we would survive our present ordeal, it would result, not from any favored treatment from a benign and all-powerful Deity, but from the skill, courage and persistence of the man in the cockpit beside me, and from the rugged machinery that our dedicated aircraft designers and engineers at The Bristol Aircraft Company had built for us. My faith was in my fellow man, not in any remote and impartial God.

I stared through the front windshield, and I could see Verna's face in the rising sea, and the tears on her cheeks on the day we stood by my Vauxhall sedan just before I'd left for final Bombing and Gunnery School in Scotland. That was the last time I'd held her in my arms.

The captain's voice put an end to my reverie.

"Seems to be working," His voice sounded somewhat less strained.

I glanced at the temperature gauge. It was still above the red line but incredibly, the engine kept on going. For several more minutes, I watched the captain working with the boost control. Despite his methodical cycling of the plus-9-boost control and the carefully planned intervals when, at 500 feet, he would turn it off, the temperature gauge remained above the red line. Each time he applied the extra power, I listened closely to the sound of the engine, trying to detect any change in its roughness. There was none. We droned steadily on.

Was I wrong? Would we by some miracle make it after all? I began to busy myself with my charts and my navigation calculator. I began to hope again.

With our sole crippled engine alternately racing and resting, and with our ears always straining for additional roughness, we continued to undulate our way across that seemingly limitless expanse of restless water.

Our overheated engine somehow withstood the series of abuses to which the captain had subjected it, and our eyes remained glued to the horizon ahead. When, after almost an hour, the faint outline of the Yemen coast began to take form along the horizon, I could barely contain my excitement. I turned to Pike. Again that slight smile. He nodded his head as if to acknowledge that yes, we were probably going to make it. Eventually, as we approached the shoreline, Pike banked the aircraft very slightly to starboard, to coax it around to a more southerly course. He turned toward me to call for a revised ETA, his manner and expression now noticeably more relaxed. We made our way south along the Yemen beaches, flying just a few hundred feet above pristine sand and rocky outcroppings. Despite the fact that the sound of our sole engine was now noticeably rougher, the chances of making a fairly survivable landing on one of the broad expanses of sand below seemed promising.

A few minutes before our projected arrival time at our home base, Pike spoke again.

"Check the wheels."

I struggled with the manual control lever, which offered an emergency alternative to the powered system for lowering the undercarriage, but nothing happened. Pike then checked for operation of the landing flaps. Again no response. We had lost all our hydraulic fluid. The aircraft would have to land without wheels or the help of flaps to slow our landing speed.

As I was considering the likely influence of those handicaps on our prospects for a safe landing, the unmistakable outline of the central buildings at our Khormaksar base came into view. Oh, what a wondrous sight! I turned to Pike with a relief that I am sure must have shone right out of my eyes, and the nascent grin that twitched the corners of his mouth at that moment will stay with me always. It lit up the cockpit.

But the challenges to our safe arrival were not quite over. As we turned toward the stretch of sand that served as the station's landing area, our single operating engine, that rugged and badly abused assembly of precision components that for nearly two hours had been our sole means of staying aloft, coughed twice and grew silent.

There was nothing now. The airplane had become a large, very heavy glider—a dead bird, wings spread wide, but dead just the same. Pike trimmed the airplane for best glide ratio. He banked gently to the left for our final approach. The rush of air over our wings and fuselage was all that could be heard as he guided our crippled war-bird toward the vast stretch of sand that served as our runway. I held my breath as, with our air-speed just above the stall, we approached the sea wall. We cleared this last obstacle by just a few feet and seconds later a sharp jolt, and a loud and continuing scraping noise as the aircraft skidded on its belly across the flat expanse of the airfield, signaled the end of our mission.

Sand poured into the cockpit, sending charts and navigation equipment flying in all directions as it filled the area around our legs. Outside, clouds of sand blocked all visibility as our forward speed bled off and we came to a grinding stop. I was conscious of a surge of relief coupled with profound admiration; relief that we were home, safe, and in one piece; and admiration for what I would later remember as the finest example of courage, skill, and airmanship that it would ever be my privilege to witness in all my wartime service.

"Out quickly!" Squadron Leader Pike released his seatbelt, opened the hatch and slid down the wing, all in one quick series of motions. I was dazed and pre-occupied with the task of recovering my navigation bag. Rummaging around in the sand, I eventually hauled it up from under my seat, and staggered toward the door.

"Come on—get out!" It was Pike again, concerned for the safety of his crew.

My head cleared, and I scrambled to obey. Outside, we made our way across the flat hard sand toward the white block-and-stucco single-story building that served as our squadron headquarters. Some fifty feet away, the three of us, S\Ldr Pike, Geordie, and I, paused to take a final look at the smoking ruin that had brought us home in one piece.

Then I stooped and kissed the ground of that remote outpost of my homeland, and I savored the rasp of the hot sand on my mouth.

THREE

Coventry, England
Spring 1937

I saw Verna for the first time through the stockroom window. Now and then, I'd catch a glimpse of her—a tall girl with chestnut hair, styled with a small group of curls at the side, like a bow or a small bunch of grapes. That unusual hair-do fascinated me almost as much as the smiling face it crowned.

The General Electric Company had transferred me to its Ford Street, Coventry Branch, as part of a promotion. At the tender age of eighteen years, I reveled in the title of 'charge hand,' and one of my jobs was to keep the production line well supplied with parts. Now and then, I'd go to the stockroom window for supplies, and I'd see Verna being served at the opposite window. Sometimes, I'd make up my mind to smile at her through those two windows, but when the chance came, I just never managed to pull it off. Once in a while, our eyes would meet across the width of the stockroom and I'd wimp-off, weak-kneed— even, on occasion, forgetting the supplies I'd come for.

Weeks and months went by and there seemed no way I could bring myself to approach her. At the end of the day I'd watch her walking off alongside the building and I'd be captivated by her graceful swinging stride, not able to tear my eyes away until she turned the corner at Ford Street. I'd tell myself that the next day, positively, I'd march into the shipping department and invite her to lunch.

The next days came and went one after another, but no lunch; nothing. Edith Layton's big son just didn't have the courage. Were it not for a happy stroke of fate, we might have continued working on opposite sides of the GEC Ford Street stockroom for a long time to come without getting any closer view of each other than that afforded by those well-spaced windows.

The happy intervention of fate came one evening when I went to the Saturday night dance at the Rialto Casino in Coundon. In earlier days, I would probably have spent that evening with my buddy Doug Philips, whose breezy extrovert personality and outdoor sportsman's enthusiasm for any new experience always ensured that our outings together would never be dull. But a few months ago Doug had got himself a girlfriend, and things had naturally changed, and although he and Ida invariably invited me to join their Saturday night outings I rarely felt inclined to make up a threesome. In any case, on this particular occasion, Doug and Ida were going to visit Ida's parents, so I decided I'd better find something to do with my evening.

I didn't know that Verna lived in Coundon and I don't remember why I picked that particular place. I sat at a table in one corner of the huge hall and idly watched the dancers circling under the revolving kaleidoscope of colored lights. A slow foxtrot played and I found myself captivated by the combined effect of the rhythmic movement on the dance-floor and the interplay of colored lights reflected from sequins and evening gowns of every style and texture.

I didn't recognize her at first. I was simply enjoying the music and the relaxing atmosphere, not really seeing individual faces or forms. Suddenly I found myself watching a girl, somewhat taller than those around her, twirling with her partner toward the center of the ballroom. I saw a floral gown of autumn colors and a graceful form that I seemed to recognize—and then I saw the nut-brown hair curled at the side of her forehead. She was here. Rainbows danced.

But not for long. My wits together again, I asked myself whether I was any better off watching her from a distance in the Rialto Casino than at the Ford street stockroom window. I went off to the bar and ordered a good stiff scotch-and-soda, drained it in a few gulps, strode back into the ballroom, and made straight for Verna's table. She looked up just as I came within a few feet of her chair. I stopped in my tracks. She looked directly at me. It was too much. I walked right on past her and slunk away, back to my own table.

In the end, shame and the dance-band leader came to my rescue. In those times, the M.C. or the bandleader might sometimes announce a 'gentlemen's excuse me,' or a 'ladies choice' number. On these occasions, to dance with a man or woman of one's choice, one simply had to walk up to him or her while a dance was in progress, tap the partner on the shoulder and take that partner's place. The next number gave men the choice, and before I knew it, Verna was there on the dance floor again, wrapped up in a tango with a tall, elegant-looking young man. This had to be my chance—a once-in-a-lifetime opportunity. Even a human jellyfish had to see that. But a tango? Couldn't it have been a nice little quickstep or a slow foxtrot? Or even an old-fashioned waltz?

It was tango or nothing. The evening would soon come to a close. People would be leaving. Verna would be leaving! Even if I tripped over my own feet and Verna's gown, too, it had to be now or never. I got up, glassy eyed but resolute, marched over to the handsome couple and tapped the back of her partner's swaying shoulders.

It was done. The elegant young man stepped graciously aside. Before I knew it, I found my left hand taking Verna's right, and my right arm gently encircling her waist. The rest of the world faded from view, and I was there, holding Verna.

I smiled. She smiled.

We danced.

When I came down from the clouds and found Verna in my arms, swaying to the tempo of the music with her clear blue eyes looking right at me—I saw that she was even taller than I'd thought, perhaps my own height or very close. Somehow that discovery unnerved me and I found myself wondering whether I should get lifts for my shoes if I were to have any hope of attracting her. But before the thought had a chance to crystallize, the dance had ended and I'd escorted Verna back to her seat to rejoin her friends. I thanked her and retreated to my table at the other side of the room. For the next couple of numbers I sat watching the dancers. Soon, I lost myself in romantic thoughts about what might follow this evening's happy encounter. I watched the ever-changing patterns of colored light, splashing across the swirling sea of faces below. Not real people any more, just harlequins with multi-hued masks drifting in and out of the shadows to the rhythm of the orchestra. Then I saw her again, gliding past my table to the rhythm of a slow foxtrot. As she became aware of my eyes following her around, she turned her head and looked directly at me, just as she had at the table. Her eyes widened to light up her face and I could see that the rose-tinted cheeks of her lovely oval face were flushed and glowing. She continued to hold my gaze until her partner had whisked her out of range.

My heart pounded. I had to do something; time to take courage again. When the orchestra leader announced the next number—a slow waltz—I went quickly to her table and, with an air of confidence I did not feel, I bowed slightly in front of her chair.

"Would you care to dance, Verna?"

Radiant and gracious, she rose from her chair, and soon we were part of the now thickening crowd of couples on the floor. Tentatively, I put my cheek against hers.

31

Then, as she didn't show any sign of disapproval, I held her in this manner for longer and longer periods and, for the most part, we danced in silence.

As the orchestra began the reprise of the main theme of the waltz, I remembered something else the bandleader had said. He'd not simply announced that this would be a slow waltz; he'd said it would be the *last* waltz. I snapped out of my blissful reverie and blurted it out—"May I see you home Verna?"

"Certainly," she replied.

Oh boy. What a night!

Unfortunately, the distance from the Rialto Casino to Verna's home at 22 Fowler Road could not, by any stretch of the imagination, be described as 'far,' and on that particular evening the walk seemed to be over almost before it had begun. We sauntered in a manner that would have left the casual observer in some doubt as to whether we were in motion at all. There was no way to drag it out further. We were there at number 22 already, and since Verna was going to use the back door, we stopped to say our goodnights in the closed passageway that ran along the side of the house to the rear entrance. I thanked her for brightening my evening and moved a little closer to her. Gazing at her upturned face, I was torn between the desire to kiss her goodnight and the fear of offending her upon such short acquaintance.

Instead of taking that particular chance, I asked her if I might see her again, whereupon she laughed and reminded me that since we were working in neighboring departments, my chances of seeing her again were pretty good. I felt myself blushing as I mumbled something about that not being exactly what I had in mind. In my confused and immature mind, I interpreted her laughter as a combination of ridicule and rejection. I took her hand and held it briefly.

Then I turned and walked away.

"Goodnight Verna."

"Goodnight."

Regardless of the dubious outcome of this wonderful evening, the ice had been broken. We were at least on speaking terms. Eventually, I got over the blues that my fragile ego had inflicted upon me, and I waited for her one evening when work was over. When she came out of the back entrance of the shipping department, I waved to her from across the covered entryway. I walked over to join her as she made her way toward the Ford street gates, and we fell in step together.

I waited with her at her bus stop, casting about in my mind for the right thing to say.

"Verna, it's good to see you- I mean, uh, I hope I didn't tread on your toes too much—at the dance, that is."

She laughed. "You don't see me hobbling, do you?" Then, turning to look at me directly, she added more quietly,

"I enjoyed dancing with you very much."

Glancing to my right, I saw the Coundon bus turning into Ford Street and approaching the stop where we were standing. In moments she would be gone.

"Verna, would you like to see the Count of Monte Christo," I blurted.

She looked surprised. "Who's he?" she asked.

"No, I mean the adventure film at the Gaumont Theater."

The bus pulled alongside the curb. Verna turned and began moving with the line to get on board.

"It's with Robert Donat," I added. "He's very good."

She mounted the entrance platform and the bus began to pull away from the curb.

"That would be nice," she called over her shoulder.

"On Saturday; I'll pick you up at seven," I yelled as I ran alongside.

I stood there waving to her as if she had just boarded the Queen Mary for a world-wide tour. Then, as the bus turned onto Far Gosford Street, I turned and walked back to where my bicycle was parked.

I felt the cool October air embrace me as I rode home. I began to whistle softly.

FOUR

Aden, Early 1941

Noise and excitement assailed me as I strolled into the sergeants' mess just after sundown. I saw Jack Novis, number two's navigator on our morning raid, sitting near the bar with three other aircrew chaps. He waved his arms, motioning me to join them. I walked over to the bar, got myself a Stella beer, and joined Jack's table.

"Hey, Turner, you want to hear the latest?"

"Sure. What can you tell me to brighten my day?"

"We're off in ten days—leaving this hell-hole."

"How do you know?"

"It's on the notice board. Go take a look."

"No, I'll take your word for it." I sat back, contemplating this revelation. "Boy, that's pretty good news. Do you know where we're going?"

"No, just that we're going, the whole bloody squadron, so you'd better not get yourself into any more scrapes like today if you want to come with us. I don't know what possessed Pike to go back for more punishment."

"I thought you'd follow us around."

"No, we lost you after the raid and assumed you'd gone down, or that we'd eventually catch up with you if you hadn't. I bet you were mighty thrilled to be a part of that action, Turner."

I looked steadily at Jack, wondering how to respond. In a moment the words came out. "As a matter of fact, I was petrified."

Wally Goodrich, lanky and thin-faced, was Geordie's counterpart in Blenheim number two. He regarded me with his usual puzzlement. "But Turner, everybody's knees tremble when the show's over, but while you're in the thick of it, it's got to be exciting."

"There's a difference Wally, a big difference. A navigator in a strafing raid has the worst of all worlds. He's in the middle of the action and the mayhem, and he has nothing to do. Navigators in most other situations fly in bombers, and when they're over the target and the sparks are flying, they're concentrating on their bombing run, passing course correction instructions to the pilot and guiding the flight slightly right or left as they peer through their bombsights and with thumb on the release button, wait for the precise moment to squeeze and let it all go. That's exciting, Wally. For those few minutes of the bombing run, the navigator is in his element. He's in command of the aircraft. But if you have no bombs to drop and no guns to fire; if in the middle of it all, with enemy bullets tearing your plane apart, and maps and charts flying everywhere, all you have in your hand is a pencil . . ." I looked around the table, then I said quietly,

"I can tell you that for me, it's . . . it's bit much, that's all."

After a moment, Jack spoke again. "So you think your chief should have come home instead of making that second run?"

"No, Jack. I've had time to think about that, and for what it's worth, I think he made the right decision. Oh, I was shit-scared at the time all right, and it took every bit of self-discipline I could muster to keep my mouth shut. I had the urge to yell at him and tell him something. I don't know what, but something. But no, he was taking a calculated risk to make sure we'd do as much damage as possible while we were there. Don't forget, in most cases, that's no more than the standard risk—the enemy almost always knows you're coming. Now that we're safely home, I'm very glad he did it, of course."

I looked around at the pensive faces at the table again. "Come on chaps, cheer up. After all . . . we're all expendable, aren't we?"

Wally scratched his head and got that puzzled look again. "Yes, I suppose the powers-that-be knew what they were doing when they gave the navigator the bomb-aimer's job as well. Lying down there at the bombsight keeps him from shitting himself while they're over the target."

All heads turned toward the door as Eric Cruttenden came striding in, arms waving above his head to call for quiet. Before enlisting, Eric had been a sales representative for Seagers, a prominent gin manufacture. About ten years my senior, he seemed to have taken it upon himself to keep an eye out for my welfare, and when I got myself into scrapes of one sort or another, he would be there just in case the going got too rough. Crut was taller and heavier than I and most of the other aircrew chaps in the squadron, and there weren't too many of them who would choose to cross him. He wouldn't interfere if there was a fair fight in the offing, but when, occasionally, my ready tongue would provoke justifiable umbrage on the part of several of our crowd, such as the time in the mess when I insisted that men who wore jewelry other than just a wedding ring were sissies; or the occasion when I told a chap from Yorkshire that his accent was worse than Cockney, Crut would get involved to even the odds and threaten to break a few heads if there should be any mass mayhem afoot. Or the time when I told an Oxford graduate that his accent was simply an affectation and a distortion of the King's English. Crut's deep voice and black Prussian moustache with its upturned and neatly waxed ends, managed to discourage most unsporting forays.

"Quiet everybody. I just got the news from the adjutant. We've got mail! We can pick it up at Admin, until 2200 hours." Then he walked over to me. "I picked yours up while I was getting mine, Turner. It's over in the hut on your bed." He held up his hand. "No, no, don't thank me. Buy me a beer instead. Then let's go eat."

My stomach churned in anticipation as I went to the food counter for sausage-and-mash and canned peaches.

Back at the table, Crut started in on me. "What's up, Turner? What's on your mind?" He could read me like a book. "You can't wait to get to that mail, can you?"

"Did I get much?"

"Just a card. It was from that whore you visited in Staverton, I think."

I grabbed an apple from the fruit basket on the table and threw it at him.

He warded off the missile with the back of his hand and grinned at me. "You'll just have to exercise that famous self-discipline of yours and wait and see. Come on, settle down Turner, or you'll choke on your bangers."

Somehow, I resisted the temptation to rush back to our hut to find out whether I'd received anything from Verna. I went through the meal in a daze, and when the last of the dinner hour was over, and the chatter had subsided, instead of rushing ahead, I forced myself to stroll back to our billet with the crowd.

I sat on my bed, my back against my kitbag, and picked up my mail. A bumper crop to be sure—a parcel from home; another from Elaine Stemmet in Cape Town, and three letters. Two were from mother, and a third envelope in Verna's unmistakable handwriting was post-marked Coundon. A feast for the famished.

Leaving the parcels for the morning, I resisted the temptation to start with Verna's letter, and opened mother's first. All was well and the tone entirely cheerful, though she was pretty fed up with all that bombing. "In fact," she wrote, "I and most of the others in Stoke (our

39

suburb of Coventry), have had enough of these constant back and forth trips to the shelters every night. We're fed up with it. We just stay in our beds these days, and put our trust in God. If our houses get a direct hit, that will be that, but mostly, they won't, and we'll be okay, so don't worry." The City Center, she wrote, had pretty much disappeared, but there were plenty of corrugated iron Nissen pre-fab buildings springing up to keep them going with food supplies and other essentials, and she could still go to the pub around the corner and get a bottle of ale when she wanted it. Hitler could go fly a kite. "Mark my words," she concluded, "his turn will come!"

A heart-warming letter to say the least, but the next one was not quite as feisty. My brother, Archie, in his eagerness to do something for the war effort, but unable to qualify physically for active service, had decided to join ENSA, the outfit for entertaining the troops. As an accomplished pianist, he was accepted at once, and with the honorary rank of captain and wearing the regulation battle dress, he was already on his way to the continent with his group.

This was of grave concern to my mother. She knew that living conditions in war-time European lodgings, and the occasional need to live under canvas, would tax her arthritic son's physical resources to the limit. Since the time of his birth, Archie had suffered from arthritis and an acute sensitivity to damp weather conditions.

"Just pray for my Archie," she wrote. "He's going to need it."

Yes, I would certainly do that.

Finally, I picked up Verna's letter, stared awhile at the pale blue 'Postagram' envelope, and turned it over several times. I hesitated another few moments. Then I slit it open.

"My darling, it's only two weeks since you left, but I still can't get used to being without you . . ."

I devoured the words. I put the letter down and lay back against my kitbag. Things were all right between us, and that was all that mattered.

Someone outside yelled, "Lights out!" Goodrich heaved himself out of his bunk, loped down to the end of the hut and flipped the switch. I drifted back to my first date with Verna.

FIVE

England 1937

I've whistled myself into darkness. Not the darkness of that Saturday evening, but the darkness that comes when memory fails—when one strains every nerve to recall and etch in ones mind every detail of a magical and dreamlike episode that one has lived through and is afraid of losing. In the course of the days and evenings that followed those moments at the bus stop with Verna I immersed myself in her relaxed and light-hearted ability to look upon each new day as a flowing river of happy adventures, along which she would float serenely. As I look back on those times, well-defined occasions come to mind with great clarity and in considerable detail, so that I remember facial expressions and tones of voice, colors in a room, and even the clothes people might have been wearing at the time. Then there are other intervals that are hazy and dreamlike, as if they never really happened, regardless of the fact that they included many precious and important moments. Such is the case as I now continue this narrative, for the whistling fades, and the ride home has no ending.

One special incident comes to me from that first date at a movie together. Verna had gone down the aisle to the ladies room as I sat watching a newsreel. Later, as she walked back again, I could see her form silhouetted against the bright rays of light reflected from the screen. She walked with her customary swinging stride as if she were modeling a gown at a fashion show. Enchanted by her grace, I could not take my eyes from her. A wondrous moment—then it was gone. I have only a vague recollection of the film we saw on that first date, and of the rest of that evening and those that followed, until I was invited to Verna's home for the first time. Then all becomes clear once more.

I suppose every new girl or boy that a teenaged son or daughter brings home for the first time, is subject to special scrutiny by each member of the family, probably so that a broad range of opinions is available to bring to bear on the post-visit evaluation that must surely follow. Even at my tender age of eighteen years, I was aware of this procedure and I was expecting to feel this sort of scrutiny when, a few weeks after our first evening together, we arranged that I would come to Verna's home to pick her up for another outing together. On that particular Friday evening, there was no hurry. We didn't have to concern ourselves with the starting times of any of the local motion pictures, nor any other special event. We were simply going to visit the local pub to join my pal Doug Phillips and his girl-friend Ida and, over a beer or two, plan a Midland Red bus tour of Warwick and Kenilworth castles. We'd agreed that I would be at

Verna's place at about 7pm, but as I parked my BSA Spider 350 motorbike at the curbside at 22 Fowler Rd, I noted that it was barely six-thirty. Dare I knock on their door so early? I realized that there was no way Verna would be ready yet, and that she might not look kindly on my early arrival. On the other hand, I was looking forward to the opportunity to spend a little time with her family.

I unhooked the latch of the front gate and made my way along the garden path to the small porch sheltering the front door. Standing there with the brass knocker within reach, I felt a trickle of perspiration running down the back of my neck. Would they like me? What if they didn't like me at all? What if they were suspicious of my intentions, and were wondering why a callow eighteen-year-old youth was pursuing their beautiful daughter and sister?

Verna had discussed her many siblings with me on several recent occasions, perhaps to prepare me for the close inspection with which I would in due course have to deal. I went over the line-up in my mind. Bessie Ogleby, the eldest at twenty-two, was engaged to Norris Wood. Verna, nearing nineteen, and six months older than I, was next. Then there was vivacious sixteen-year-old Flossy whom Verna described as the drama girl, followed by Olive, just fifteen. Ten-year old Elma, who according to Verna was the future blond-bombshell of the family, was next. She and her eight-year-old brother, Donald, were the small-fry of the family. I went over the list again in my mind, wondering how it would go with them.

Well, I would soon find out. I straightened my tie again and took a deep breath. I raised the brass knocker above the letter-box, and rapped twice.

Almost immediately, a tall, shapely brunette greeted me at the door. After a short appraisal by her clear blue eyes as they swept over me smoothly, she smiled.

"Hello Howard, I'm Flossie. Come in."

"I, ah, thank you Flossie. I hope I'm not disturbing you. I know I'm early."

"No you're not— disturbing us I mean," she replied. "But you'll have to wait around a bit."

From the small vestibule in which we were now standing, Flossie led me through another doorway into a large living room where a delightful array of long, shapely arms and legs greeted me. The scene reminded me of pictures I'd seen of vaudeville theatre dressing rooms. I saw then that Flossie was wearing a sort of sleeveless jacket over her slip, and had just been ironing the dress she evidently intended to wear that evening. Her younger sister, Olive, similarly dressed, and seated in an armchair at the left of the fireplace, was busy sewing buttons on a white blouse. Neither sister seemed concerned or self-conscious about their lack of outer garments. Olive waved me over to an armchair by the fireplace.

"Since father is not here, why don't you make yourself comfortable in his chair," she said. Elma, who'd been occupying that venerable seat, smiled at me with star-like eyes and moved to a wooden stool at the other side of the fireplace. Both children seemed engrossed in their homework.

No ceremony. As I settled myself comfortably between the two children, I looked around again and caught Olive's eye. She'd evidently been crying, and tears were still glistening on her cheeks. She became aware of my concerned glance. Then she laughed and explained that she'd had a tiff with her girl-friend and was crying more in anger than in sorrow. She laughed again and began to make a joke of her unhappiness, so that slowly, her immediate misfortunes seemed to melt away, to be replaced by her interest in her sister's boyfriend. Flossie, by contrast, was muttering impatiently and tugging at the dress she was ironing.

"I'm already late for my date," she grumbled, "and this thing isn't looking any better at all for my efforts."

I asked her if I could help, and fortunately she found that offer quite funny. At any rate, she stopped being desperate and simply dragged the dress off the ironing board.

"That will have to do," she told me with a sniff.

Mrs. Ogleby, wiping her hands on the apron at her waist, bustled in from the kitchen, blowing at strands of gray-streaked dark hair, that were falling persistently in front of her kindly but tired blue eyes. Smiling warmly, she came forward and shook my hand.

"Verna told me you were coming," She looked up at me, "and I'm very pleased to meet you." Then she added, "Would you like a cup of tea Howard, while you're waiting for Verna to get ready?"

"Yes, thank you Mrs. Ogleby. May I come and help you make it?"

"No, no, young man. Just this once you're going to be the honored guest and you'd better make the most of it. You'll be permitted to help with the tea next time."

I already felt at home.

Soon, I became a regular visitor to number 22 and I began to learn a bit about Mr. Ogleby's work as a pattern maker and his considerable patience and attention to detail with his projects at work or at home in the garden. He was a down-to-earth, straightforward and uncomplicated man and I enjoyed my occasional discussions with him. Somehow, he made me feel older and more responsible than I usually felt about myself, perhaps because he listened to my ideas and opinions just as attentively as I listened to him. Mrs. Ogleby, too, though much over-worked in her daily life, was always ready with a warm welcome whenever I turned up. No fuss, no pretense—just a friendly smile and a joke or two to let me know that my visits were never inconvenient.

I began to get to know the young ones, Elma and Donald, and in the course of my second visit, Elma, who routinely occupied her father's chair when he was absent, again beckoned me over to her fireside throne. She slipped onto the stool at its side and motioned me to take her place.

"You can be my father for now," she said, batting the lashes of her sparkling blue eyes at me, "and help me with my homework."

Once again, I settled myself comfortably in her father's armchair, and with Donald and Elma sitting beside me, I turned my attention to the task at hand. The warmth of their simple welcome had touched me, but more than that, I was conscious of the closeness of this appealing group of siblings, and of their security. I was suddenly aware of the absence of a father from my own life, and how much I'd taken my brother and my mother for granted. I spent little time these days with either of them, and seldom made a point of thanking my mother for the wonderful meals she cooked for the three of us every day. Nor had I ever paid much attention to my brother or his day-to-day activities and interests. In fact, apart from his developing skills as a pianist, I hardly knew what his interests were. As I immersed myself more and more in the domesticity around me, I resolved that I would do something about that.

Those weeks that, imperceptibly, turned into months, were heady times for me. Although, on the one hand, I repeatedly reminded myself that I was too young and inexperienced to be thinking about any kind of serious attachment, it was becoming increasingly clear to me every day that I was really in love with Verna. Not just infatuated, fascinated or dazzled. I was a total goner, hopelessly and deeply in love. Whenever, during the week, an opportunity presented itself, we visited each other's homes and shared our time with each other's families. On Saturdays we went sightseeing, or camping alongside the river Avon at Stratford, swimming and cooking our meals on Primus stoves. When we stayed within the Coventry area, we played tennis and visited outdoor swimming pools, and went to see the most popular motion pictures or plays in the evenings.

Our visits to the Coventry Opera House were, for me, among the most memorable of our times together, for they permitted me to share my secret artistic passion with the girl I loved so dearly. On the occasion of our first visit, as I sat there with Verna, watching the actors perform 'Arsenic and Old Lace,' I was entranced. It was life. It was everything. Totally captivated, I felt myself up there on the stage, identifying with the male lead and playing his part, and I told myself that whatever happened, I must do this. I must become an actor.

On the way home after the show, I told Verna of my secret passion. Recalling those days of my childhood and youth, I began to pour it all out; how the longing to be on the stage had so often occupied my childhood dreams, and why I had kept it a secret and had never acted upon it.

"Parents naturally do all they can to encourage their children in activities where they show the most interest," I told her, "and while that's as it should be, it sometimes results in the masking of a true ambition by a secondary one. As a child, I'd always shown an interest in mechanical toys and Meccano model building sets, so those were the gifts I got when Christmas and my birthdays came around," I paused. "But it was our occasional visits to school plays and to the theater that really enthralled me. I didn't reveal it to anyone because my brother and I already had our problems and got into fights at school because of our nice neat clothes and short pants. Raising us by herself, mother did the very best for us she could, but she didn't realize that children need to be dressed like their peers and boys need to be dressed like other boys. I didn't want to make matters worse, so I didn't do any play-acting or get involved in school productions because in those days it was in any case considered a sissy thing for boys to do. Play-acting was for girls, so I smothered my true interest in that sort of thing and concentrated on all the things that boys were supposed to be interested in. When I wasn't out hiking or biking or playing football with my friends, I played with Meccano sets and trains, and buried my true interest."

I felt the old excitement rising in me as I continued.

"Verna my darling, tonight is the first time I've told anyone about my secret dream, but the way that play affected me tonight, I feel that some day I'll have to find out what my chances are. I just have to. I . . ." She cut me off.

"Do it Howard," she said. "And do it now. At least get it out of your system, or you will always wonder about it. You may never be truly happy until you bring it out in the open."

The following evening Verna had plans to go with her elder sister to a gym class, so we would not be spending the evening together. I used the opportunity to return to the Opera House alone to see the play a second time. In the course of the next ten days, I saw it yet again. Shortly thereafter, I phoned the director of the Opera House at his headquarters in Corporation Street, and made an appointment to see him, and a day or two later I was sitting across from him in his office.

He was friendly but firm. "I wish I could help you Howard, but we are a production company and we have no opportunity to work with people who have no experience. If you get yourself at least a year or so of acting school, it's possible that we could sometimes try you out in bit parts. But it's a long hard road and even if you're dedicated, it's not a promising way to make a living. If you do decide to get some formal training, by all means come back and see us and we'll have another talk."

That settled that. I came to my senses and chided myself for not realizing that there would be financial problems, anyway. How could I possibly go off to some acting school when a good part of my present wage was needed to help with household expenses at home? Out of the question. I thanked the production director for seeing me and told him that one day I would be back to see him again.

Despite the cold reality that I had now been made aware of, I felt better for having brought the dream of my childhood into the light and shared it with Verna. In any case, I had a whole life ahead of me to re-visit my thespian inclinations. It could wait.

For the present, my world was full enough. It had become a dancing, tingling, roller-coaster playground in which I traveled to exhilarating heights when I was able to see Verna and know that all was well with us, and a plunge into stomach churning uncertainty during the in-between days and evenings when I could not see her. Whenever my immature and jealous nature would give rise to any strains in our relationship, sleep was out of the question, and I suffered agonies of self reproach until I was able to hold her in my arms again. With the benefit of hindsight, I found myself more and more amazed that Verna had shown such tolerance on those occasions— always so ready to forgive and forget when I would finally come to my senses and apologize for my childish behavior.

The months flew by and soon Christmas was upon us. The GEC Christmas celebration was always an event to look forward to. It took place in the Stoke works ballroom, right there on Telephone road. Christmas cake, mince pies and a variety of other deserts made up an appealing spread at one end of the ballroom, and a lively dance-band performed on the broad stage at the other end. In an adjacent alcove, wine, beer and spirits were offered at half their usual prices, and soft drinks were free.

Since GEC employees were permitted to bring one guest each, Verna and I had invited Doug and Ida, and we'd managed to secure a sizable table in one of the corners at the stage end of the room. Verna positively glowed that evening. Radiant in an ice-blue floor-length gown that clung seductively to her shapely figure, she nevertheless seemed oblivious to all the admiring glances from her co-workers sharing the festivities with us. In my view, however, she was always much too friendly with members of the opposite sex. She had girl-friends, too, of course, but she seemed to lavish her smiles and attention far more on her male co-workers of any age, than on their female counterparts.

Would I call it flirting? I always found it difficult to tell with women, but if it wasn't that, it was certainly pretty close—and it seemed especially so on this Christmas party evening. I found my mood darkening as she readily accepted invitations to dance whenever a co-worker bowed at our table and asked her for that privilege.

"Why do you have to say yes every time someone asks you for a dance, Verna? The way things are going, we shan't have much time for dancing ourselves, shall we?"

Verna sighed. "They're my friends and co-workers and I get very little opportunity to socialize with them."

"But you see them every day. Isn't that enough?"

"I see them at work on and off in the daytime and I see you most evenings. Would you prefer the reverse? Come on, smile for me my darling, and let's get on that floor right now." She flashed me one of her indulgent smiles—and we danced.

Later in the evening, a good looking co-worker who had already danced with her earlier, approached our table and bowed before Verna.

"May I have the pleasure again, Verna?"

Verna glanced at me fleetingly. "I'd love to," she replied.

I sloped off to the bar, leaving Doug and Ida to themselves. After a couple of Scotches and soda, I returned to our table and danced with Ida. Thereafter, I approached other tables where the girls seemed the prettiest, and danced with whoever was available. I did not dance again with Verna that evening until the last waltz, and even then, I danced in sullen silence.

The ride home brought no negative reaction from Verna, and she behaved as if the evening had been a total success. When, still smarting, I gave her a perfunctory goodnight kiss she pulled me to her again. "Let's try that once more," she said.

And in the simple brushing of her soft lips across my face and on my eyelids, all my frustrations took flight.

But even Verna's patience had its limits, and there eventually came a point when she'd had enough of my adolescent sulking. It was a Saturday evening, and although neither Doug nor Ida was especially fond of dancing, we'd persuaded them to join us for an evening at the Rialto Casino to try it out. Verna was especially radiant that evening. Her tall, shapely figure, clad in an autumn colored gown, had become the object of overt and covert admiring glances as she moved gracefully around the dance floor. Halfway into a men's excuse-me foxtrot, a tow-headed, fresh-complexioned fellow had tapped me on the shoulder and taken Verna from me. Then, later in the evening, as a new number was being announced, he'd come to our table, bowed in front of Verna, and asked her to dance.

This was too much for me. I leapt to my feet before she could reply. Totally overlooking the fact that this was exactly how I had behaved on that memorable occasion when I had taken Verna home for the first time, I glared at the intruder.

"Can't you see that this is a private party, my friend," I growled at him.

"If you like to dance, why don't you bring a partner of your own instead of crashing other people's parties?"

"Don't you think it's up to Verna to decide whether or not she would like to dance with me?" Tow-head replied calmly.

Verna! He'd used her name. How dare he!

"Let's go outside and I'll teach you some etiquette," I snarled at him.

"No need for that," he said without raising his voice. "If Verna wants to dance with me, we'll dance. If not, I shall not trouble you or your overbearing ego any further."

I saw red. I swung my clenched fist at Tow-head with all my weight behind it. Tow-head, with unexpected agility, side-stepped the blow. Before I was able to regain my balance, he placed the flat of his two hands on my chest, and gave me a hard shove that knocked me right off my feet. I shook my head and, as I climbed to my feet again, I cast about for a weapon. I noted that the chair I was holding was a light cane-backed design. It would serve the purpose. I picked it up and swung it at Tow-head—and watched with considerable satisfaction as he crumpled in a heap on the floor.

The Rialto bouncer and a couple of his henchmen converged on our table, and before the hapless Tow-head could get to his feet again, we were both grabbed from behind and muscled out of the dancehall into the sobering air of that October night.

I looked around, expecting further reprisals from Tow-head, but he was nowhere to be seen. He must have decided that further involvement with a madman was not in his best interests. Moments later, Doug and Ida came to check me out, and to tell me that Verna had asked them to take her home.

When Doug and Ida and Verna had gone and I was left standing in the street feeling injured in every way, tow-head appeared out of the shadows and sauntered up to me. I noted that he was more powerfully built than I had earlier judged. I opened my mouth to say something, but he cut me off.

"You're an overbearing egomaniac," he said, "and now that we're alone, I'm going to teach you a lesson."

Without waiting for a response, he again placed the flat of his hands on my chest. I swung my left fist at him with all the energy I could muster, but again, as he had done on our first encounter, he ducked his head out of the way and simultaneously shoved, this time more forcefully than when we were going at it in the dancehall. I went sprawling on my back and hit my head on the concrete pavement. I shook my head, scrambled to my feet, and struck out again; this time with better luck. I felt the searing pain in my wrist as my fist made contact with Tow-head's face, just below his right eye. Then as his responding blow landed like a sledgehammer on my chin, I passed out.

I saw Tow-head only once after that encounter. The following morning, the nurse at the hospital where I spent that eventful night, told me I had a visitor. The now familiar stocky form strolled up to my bedside.

"They tell me you're OK," he said. "No hard feelings——at least on my part."

I glanced up at him and noted with some satisfaction that he had a fat bruise at the side of his right eye.

"No, no hard feelings. I suppose I had it coming."

For a week, Verna refused to see me, and I had great difficulty persuading her that I was going to change. I did my best to persuade her that my character was not really like that, and that my miserable behavior was just a lover's malady that would soon go away. The explanation sounded pretty weak to me as I offered it, and it didn't impress Verna at all. But, perhaps against her better judgment, she eventually decided to give me another chance.

I was truly shaken. I'd suddenly been confronted with the prospect of losing Verna—and that possibility led me to concentrate on the serious matter of growing up. I determined to tread a little more softly; to count ten more often, and be more of a true and appreciative friend. And, I decided, I would do something special, something that would impress her and serve as a sign that she was very important to me—and that I had changed. Something like the deeds of bravery that young men of ages past would do to win favor with their chosen ladies. Something.

But I was not brave, and even if I were, I couldn't think of a brave deed that I could do that would quite serve the purpose. I could not save her from anything, because she was not in any danger that I knew of, and as far as I knew, there was no unwelcome rival around to vanquish. There didn't seem to be any special material thing she wanted either, or anything that I could get for her. I could buy her flowers of course—yes I would certainly do that—but that would not be special enough for my purpose. I would have to think harder.

SIX

England 1938

The Golden Hind

The answer to my problem came quite unexpectedly. I had decided to confide in my friend Roy Flowers and seek his advice concerning my need to show Verna how much I loved her. Roy, bespectacled, mild-mannered and studious, gave an impression of maturity and wisdom beyond his years. Thick eyebrows, matching his receding black hair, served to enhance his professorial aura. One day, in the course of a visit to his home, I noticed an attractive model ship on the mantelpiece above his living-room fireplace. The small replica of Sir Francis Drake's flag-ship, the 'Golden Hind,' with its sails billowing, and all guns at the ready, fascinated me, and I began to see it in my mind, somewhat increased in size and more finely crafted. What a labor of love it would be if one were to invest the time and energy necessary to make a realistic replica of the original galleon. Not just another decorative piece fashioned from a standardized kit of parts ordered from a catalogue, but a model built by hand from the most basic raw materials.

The more I thought about it, the more it seemed to me that a hand-made model of that ship would be a worthwhile gift for Verna—an offering that would serve as an ever present reminder of my love for her. Yes, that was it. That's what I would do. I would take it slowly and methodically and work my way through the myriad component parts, fashioning each piece with loving care. As I continued to gaze at the diminutive model in front of me, I could see myself carving the hull and turning the metal gun barrels on a lathe, erecting the masts and fabricating the curved parchment sails, weaving and knotting the countless rope-ladders and endless yards of rigging.

The finished vessel was already taking shape in my mind when my friend, sitting quietly beside me and smiling indulgently, snapped his fingers in front of my eyes and brought me out of my reverie.

"Where are you my friend?"

I blinked. "Oh, sorry Roy. That model ship got me thinking. I think I'd like to make one like that for Verna. Fact is, I'm in the dog house, and if I made something like that for her, it might give her a better impression of me."

Roy peered at me over the top of his wire-rimmed glasses and chuckled. "No need to worry, old chum, I can save you the trouble. If you just go down to the art store where I got this one, you can get a complete kit of parts and a set of plans to put it together."

"No no, that's not what I want, Roy. I want to build the ship from scratch; make all the bits and pieces myself, and put 'em all together so that the finished job will be uniquely my handiwork, my creation, not just a carbon copy of every other kit-built model around. Don't you see that?" I paused to assess the effect of my words, but Roy was a good listener.

"Anything else?" he said, arching his heavy eyebrows, "I'm listening."

"Well, It's just that I'd like to get some plans or photographs for reference purposes, to ensure accuracy, but as I said, I want to build the ship myself from scratch.

Roy shook his head slowly from side to side as if convinced that I'd taken leave of my senses. Then he stood looking at me for a few long moments in a benign, almost avuncular, fashion. He opened his mouth to say something, then changed his mind and with a wave of his hand disappeared into his workroom.

In a few minutes he was back with the information on the art shop in his hand, and with a couple more of those meaningful head-shakings, he handed me the paper.

I encountered the same bewilderment when I visited the art shop a few days later. A lanky young sales assistant, whose freckled face was partly concealed by a generous swathe of yellow hair that hung over his left eye, came forward to greet me. Nigel—I think that was his name— sported a powder blue, open-necked shirt. He stared at me impassively.

"And what will it be today?" he asked.

"What will what be? The weather? I really don't know, but it looks pretty promising so far, don't you think?"

His face cracked a smile. "That was just my way of asking what I can do for you."

"Oh, I see. Well yes, as a matter of fact, you can do something for me. I want to build a model of a ship—the Golden Hind to be precise—and I'm wondering whether you can provide me with construction plans for it, or if not the plans, then perhaps a picture of it."

"That's easy. The complete drawings come with the kit. Let me get it out for you."

"No, no, you don't understand. I'm not looking for a kit. I want to build my own version of it, so it will be unique."

Nigel's visible eye stared at me in puzzlement. Then he shook his head.

"Can't be done. The plans go with the kit. You buy a kit and you get the plans, sorry." Then he added, "Beats me why anyone would want to set about carving out a whole bloody ship's hull, then go fiddling with all those bits and pieces when they're already there for you, sitting in a box." He shook his head again and the blonde swathe swung from side to side in front of his nose, emphasizing his disapproval.

I decided to change my tactics.

"Look, Nigel, I'm in the dog house with my girl-friend, and I want to do something for her, something difficult and time-consuming, something that will show her that I've put in a great deal of time and effort to create a unique gift for her. A kit-built model won't do that for me. She'll spot it at once. But if I create something that's clearly hand-made and unique, I know it will make all the difference. Come on, now, be a sport and help me out. It will really mean a lot to me."

Nigel stood there considering the matter. Then he turned and made his way to the storeroom behind him and dragged out a large cardboard carton.

"Tell you what I'll do," he said, opening the top. "I'll lend you the manual and drawings out of this kit and you can take them home and copy or photograph whatever you want. I'll trust you to have them back here in three or four days, but you'd better give me some security money just in case."

A few minutes later, I left the art store with the plans in my pocket.

All I needed now was a hull; or rather, a special piece of wood from which to make a hull. It needed to be large enough and thick enough so that the entire hull could be carved out of that single piece. And it had to be fine hard wood—mahogany or oak or some such. A piece six inches thick by six inches wide and about two feet long would do the job, and I managed to find exactly what I needed among a stack of gateposts stored in a local building contractor's warehouse.

As the model galleon began to take shape, I became more and more dedicated to my purpose. Its successful completion became very important to me, not only because of its special value as a gift for Verna, but also because I saw it in my mind as a test of persistence and patience, qualities hitherto quite foreign to my nature. Eventually the block of oak took on new life as I fashioned it into the shape of a hull. Portholes appeared along the sides, and batteries of bronze gun-barrels poked through the firing ports at deck level. I'd created the guns themselves by turning them individually on a small lathe at the General Electric Company radio works, and the shop supervisors had looked on benevolently as I spent my lunch hours shaping the small metal pieces, fussing with the rings and flutes that one sees on these ancient weapons in museums. There were sixteen of them altogether, and their appearance, bristling from the sides of the long hull, helped to make this an authentic and unique version of that venerable ship.

Then came the 'Poop' deck with its sharply angled sides and steep rear wall, and finally, the masts, sails and rigging. The sails had to be painted with St George's cross and other noble crests of the time, and I had to draw on the best of my artistic abilities to manage this particular part of the project satisfactorily. But I eventually completed it and when I'd aged the sails with sepia oil-paint, achieving the desired variations in color intensity with the judicious application of paint thinner, I was able to see that the finished job would be well worth my many weeks of concentrated effort. When, finally, the flying ensigns were set atop the ship's masts and the job done, I confess that I felt a certain pride in my handiwork and looked forward eagerly to the day when I would deliver it to its future owner.

I hand carried The Golden Hind to 22 Fowler Road one Friday evening, and when the front door was opened for me, I stepped forward and placed the ship on the living room table. Verna was there with Elma and Donald and Mr. and Mrs. Ogleby. Oh, how I relished the delighted expression on Verna's face as I peeled off the wrapping tissue to reveal my special gift with its noble bow and billowing sails, and its gaunt and antique coloring. I watched her brush tears from her eyes as she began to realize how much effort I must have put into the project, and the hug she then gave me was worth every blister and torn fingernail, every missed lunch, and every hour of toil that I'd expended on this token of my love for her.

I was deeply moved, too, by her father's reaction. This was the patient pattern- maker whose work was always painstaking and detailed, and I could tell that he was very surprised and impressed by The Golden Hind. I well remember his expression as the scene comes back to me. He studied the ship for a few moments. Then he said warmly and with unmistakable approval in his voice: "I had heard you were making a ship of some kind, Howard, but I didn't expect anything as fine as this."

My chest heaved as I reveled in the moment. I turned to Verna and took her hand in mine. "I've changed Verna. From now on things are going to be different. You'll see that I've matured, that I'm going to be much more patient."

I offered up a silent prayer that I would somehow manage to live up to that promise.

Verna with my grandfather at Sea-Mills Park, 1939

SEVEN

The Hornet

Somehow, the ship episode had given me a chance to make up for some of my earlier difficult behavior, for I believe Verna sensed that I was making a genuine effort to overcome the touchy teen age sensitivities that had plagued our developing relationship. There followed a period of wonderful times as I learned more and more about the Ogleby family, spent more time with Verna's brother and sisters around me, sometimes participating in lengthy discussions with Elma and Donald about their school-day ups and downs. And we made good use of that haven for romantic and quiet times together—the summerhouse at the bottom of the garden. Gradually, I came to know Verna's older sister Bessie and her boyfriend Norris, who, with their more mature personalities helped me, by example, to achieve a little more maturity myself. Soon Verna and I were going out together with Bessie and Norris, not often, just now and then, and I looked forward with contentment to those occasions.

But the building of the Golden Hind was not my only hobby at the time. One of my older friends at the GEC factory in Stoke had indicated that he planned to sell his sports car, a 1932 Wolseley Hornet. A green four-seat convertible, its long sleek contour appealed to my adventurous nature. I cannot remember how I managed to get together the eighteen pounds purchase price that I needed to make the deal, but in a matter of weeks the car was sitting in our garden shed, undergoing an overhaul. First I gave the engine its share of tender loving care. I fitted the six pistons with new rings, and cleaned and adjusted all the valves and tappets. I cleaned and polished practically everything under the bonnet, relined the brakes and adjusted the handbrake. Inside, I replaced the old dashboard with a hand-polished mahogany panel, and added green instrument lighting for aesthetic effect.

Finally, I replaced the collapsible canvas top with a new one, complete with a protective tonneau cover. The task occupied me for several months. I didn't drive the car much during that time, but I looked upon all the reconditioning work as a hobby in itself and I was bent on achieving an elegant transformation. For a while after I'd finished the job, I went on drives with my male friends just to show off my handiwork. Then, when I was satisfied that no more major work was necessary or desirable, I began to use my new toy to go on Friday-night joy rides with my pals, and occasionally to take Verna on jaunts into the countryside.

George screamed. "Christ! Take it easy! I'm losing my footing!"

"Sorry George," I yelled above the engine noise, "I'm not going any faster than we agreed." I eased pressure on the right pedal a little.

On an occasional Friday evening, my buddies and I would go on a spree in my sleek green car, reveling in our favorite sport. A suitable destination would be agreed upon—Leicester or Nottingham, or some other lively and not too distant town. We would set off at a good speed just for the ride and an hour or two of high-spirited fun. Then we'd make our way back again. When I say good speed, I mean that the idea was to decide on a nice brisk rate of travel and try not to slow down at all, either for bends or for corners. If one had to actually stop for a compelling reason—like a traffic light— that was OK, but otherwise we judged the adventure on our ability to maintain as constant a speed as possible.

None of us gave any thought to the extreme danger and the foolhardiness of such a venture, even though we knew that the Wolseley Hornet's track was narrower than most other sports cars of the day. That is to say, the distance between the left and right wheels was less than standard, which made the car vulnerable to tipping over when going around bends at speed. No problem. The car had quite low sides. With the canvas top down, whenever we approached a bend or corner to the left, my friend George, short and fat, would sit sideways, with his bottom perched on the side in the direction of the turn, and lean right out as far as he could, hooking his feet under the opposite seat so he wouldn't fall out.

For a corner or bend to the right, Ken Griffiths behind me, would park his leaner backside on the right side of the car and lean out in a similar manner. Between them, fat George and his neighbor in the back seat would take it in turns to lean out of whichever was the appropriate side, and the one not leaning out would act as an anchor man, helping to pin down the other's feet if he appeared to be slipping.

As we got a little practice at this bizarre sport, and as we persuaded ourselves that we were invincible, the agreed upon standard speed was raised a little at a time.

We were on our way to the Palais de Dance at Leicester, taking the last bend before the long straight slope into the City. George screamed again.

"I'm losing my footing!"

Ken swung himself off the side and threw his weight onto George's ankles and feet. For a heart-stopping moment, it seemed that his weight would not be quite enough. While he struggled to get a better grip, George, by means of some muscular resource that he was not afterward able to fully explain, managed a mighty heave that propelled his considerable torso back into the car again. As he did so, the left side of the vehicle rose off the road on its way to a certain overturn. To avert disaster, I abandoned the turn and allowed the car to continue across to the other side of the road as I braked. We were blessed that night, for the road happened to be clear of traffic at the time and, as the tires screamed their protest, we spun around more than a full turn. But we did not turn over. After a couple of hours during which we stopped at a local pub for a beer or two and some discussion about our narrow escape from disaster, we drove home—sober and somewhat subdued.

We had not, however, learned our lesson. The sleek green sports car and its driver remained—an accident waiting to happen.

One Saturday evening, a few months later, Verna and I set out on a country drive with Bessie and Norris. I well remember the pub we visited near Meriden, about eight miles west of Coventry. The road we took to reach it was not the broad straight highway that later connected Coventry with the Birmingham Airport. It was a traditional country road with a single lane in each direction, with pronounced bends where the road skirted villages en route. Just a few miles short of Meriden itself, a sharp hairpin bend, one well known by all who traveled the area and its location, was well marked with warning signs. Norris mentioned its proximity to me as we were approaching the area and I slowed the car as I caught the cautionary note in his voice. Yes, it certainly was a sharp one— especially for that narrow-tracked Hornet, and we eased around it gently.

Ten minutes later we were relaxing serenely in the lounge of the King's Arms, a congenial pub that sat back a little off the road with a wide patch of gravel in front of it to provide plenty of room for its patrons to park. There wasn't a great deal of noise and we were able to converse contentedly as we sipped our beer and exchanged our thoughts on current events and on our jobs and their ups and downs. Time slipped by as we talked and drank. It was a good evening and when Norris eventually mentioned that perhaps we should be getting on the road again, I was disappointed that this special time together had to end so soon. But leave we did.

I felt revitalized by the bracing night air as we raised the canvas top of the Hornet and cocooned ourselves comfortably inside it. Norris and I settled ourselves in the front, and Verna and Bessie took the seats behind us. I pulled out onto the Coventry–Birmingham road. The Hornet's engine purred as we gathered speed, and although there was some patchy fog, the white line in the middle of the road was always visible enough. As my eyes got more and more accustomed to the darkness and the mist, I began to drive faster. I was oblivious to all about me except the steady music of the Hornet's engine and the white line that I was tracking through the swirling mist. I eventually heard Norris's voice.

"Howard, would you care for me to drive for a while?" If there was any urgency in his tone, I certainly didn't notice it. I brushed off his suggestion.

"No thank you, Norris." I drove on, even a little faster.

When I saw the white line beginning to curve to the right, into that notorious hairpin bend, it was too late. I attempted to follow the turn, but the right wheels came up off the road immediately. There was no fat George now, to lean way out of the right side of the car to keep us level; there was no way to continue the turn without rolling over. I drove straight ahead as I braked. I remember the car running off the road over a wide grassy strip. As we careened down a steep embankment, I was conscious of the roll over to the left, first upside down, then yet farther over to a right-side up position. A large tree loomed. Oblivion.

In a while when my brief lapse into unconsciousness had passed, I saw that the Hornet, without its canvas top and with no-one in it, was right-side up and had its front end part way up the trunk of the tree we'd struck. The canvas top had been torn off as the car had rolled back onto its wheels. As it had struck the tree, we'd all been thrown out. Looking around, I saw that Norris was beginning to raise himself up from the grass where he'd been lying, and Bessie, too, was sitting on the ground rubbing her back. Verna was lying on her back and when I went to examine her more closely I was able to see that the right side of her face was covered with blood, making it impossible to determine the condition of her right eye. I had a gash on my nose and others on my shins, but that was all.

Norris was the first to stagger slowly to his feet. He looked around at the rest of us lying in the grass.

"Howard, we have to get to a phone. The best chance seems to be that house across the field. I can see the lights through the trees. Who do you think should go?

I could not speak. I was kneeling on the grass beside Verna, holding her hand. For the moment I could not move. I didn't know whether she was conscious or not and I didn't try to talk to her. I just stayed there in a sort of trance. Norris, understanding the reason for my lack of response, began to limp his way across the fields to get help. I don't remember anything after that until I found myself climbing into the back of an ambulance. Verna lay on a stretcher with Bessie by her side. Norris climbed in behind me.

No one spoke during the journey to the Coventry Hospital. We sat there with our thoughts, glancing occasionally across at Verna to see that she was comfortable. That is all I remember about the ambulance ride, except for one small but shining incident that has stayed with me always. At one point in the journey, Norris, sitting next to me, turned his head and looked at my face. He patted my leg gently several times, comforting me. In the midst of this terrible catastrophe, Norris was showing compassion for the arrogant young fool who had caused it.

We stayed with Verna at the hospital until the cut on her face had been attended to and we'd learned that her eye had escaped injury. We saw her settled comfortably in bed. I visited her whenever I got a chance during the days that followed, but I don't remember ever asking her for her forgiveness for what I had done to her. And no one, not Verna, nor Bessie or Norris, nor any member of Verna's family, ever reproached me for my recklessness. But at last, at the cost of serious injury to Verna, and a time of considerable trauma for Bessie and Norris, I had learned my lesson. What was left of the long sleek Hornet, was towed away and sold for scrap-iron for the sum of six pounds, and I did not trust myself to drive again for more than a year.

Verna's scar gradually healed and I was thankful that the accident did not seem to have damaged our relationship. When after a year or so of using buses, trains, bicycles and shank's pony, I bought another car, Verna did not seem at all reluctant to ride with me, and I was careful not to give her any cause.

In the late summer of 1938, on a blustery Saturday morning, Verna and I boarded a train for Birmingham's New Street station. Change was in the air. Leaves were falling and the moods of the season seemed to generate a certain restlessness in men, women and children alike. We'd decided to meet at the station in time for the ten thirty train, and even though I arrived more than twenty minutes early, I spotted Verna's blue raglan sleeved coat and cascading nut-brown hair, right beside the ticket office. My heart missed a beat at the vision of her loveliness and grace. For Verna, easy going, and almost always tardy, her arrival this much ahead of time must surely be a wonderful omen and an indication of her enthusiasm for our mission.

I bounded over and wrapped my arms around her. Then I held her at arms length.

"So what's this, young lady; couldn't you sleep?

She did that little thing that I knew so well, stamping her feet in a quick series of little stamps, using left and right feet alternately, like some sort of Latin dance.

"I'm so excited," she said. Then she did the little dance again.

With a compartment to ourselves, we pulled out of the Coventry station at ten thirty on the dot.

"Verna,"

"Yes."

"Why are we making this trip?"

She looked across at me, puzzled. "We're shopping for my engagement ring, aren't we?" she said.

I held out my hand, searching for hers. "Yes of course we are, but I just wanted to hear you say it, just so I'll know I'm not dreaming."

She looked across at me, suddenly serious. "Are you sure you know what you're doing, my darling?"

"Yes, my wonderful girl, I'm on a trip to Birmingham with the most gorgeous girl in the world. We're going to find the most dazzling engagement ring, and we're going to remember this day for the rest of our lives. Oh, I do so want you to be happy today, Verna." I squeezed her hand.

Her serious mood vanished as quickly as it had come. She sighed.

"Pinch me." She said dreamily.

The rhythmic drone of the carriage wheels on the rails lulled both of us into a semi stupor and we didn't talk again until we pulled into Birmingham's New Street Station. We did our shopping slowly and methodically, and although I was convinced that we'd found the perfect ring long before Verna reached the same conclusion, I reminded myself of my promise not to hurry her, and I was careful not to appear impatient in any way. We'd been at it for about an hour and a half when she made her choice; a ring with a beautiful elliptical opal surrounded by tiny diamonds. When she tried the ring on her finger, it had an almost magical effect on her. It was as if she'd been somehow transformed. Her freshness and beauty glowed as she walked back and forth in the jewelry shop, modeling the ring, splaying her fingers and waving her hand about.

"It's so beautiful," she said.

The train-ride home served as a happy and relaxing conclusion to the day's mission. I had popped the question to Verna a week earlier, and had then asked her father for her hand in marriage, so tonight would be the actual engagement ceremony. We took a bus-ride to the Bull's Head Inn on the Binley Road in the Coventry suburb of Stoke, and there, after a traditional English roast-beef dinner, to which neither of us paid much attention, and after coffee had been served, I knelt in front of her chair and slid the ring onto her finger.

I searched for words to let her know how much I loved her, and at last, they spilled out freely.

"I love you Verna, and I just can't think of anything more happy-making than spending my whole life trying to make you happy, too."

"I'll remind you of those words from time to time," she said, grinning at me impishly. Then she patted my hand and continued, "But I'm truly happy you said them."

A harvest moon bathed us in its benevolence as we eventually made our way back to Verna's home and lingered in the passageway that led through to her back garden. As I drew her to me to kiss her goodnight, she took my hand. Leading me back through the dark of the passageway, she whispered, "Let's spend a few minutes in the summerhouse. I don't want to end this wonderful day just yet."

Verna, still holding my hand, led me to the back of the house, and through the garden gate into the Ogleby backyard. Moments later, we crept into the small structure that Verna and her family fondly referred to as the summerhouse, but which, in practice, served mostly as a shelter for their garden furniture.

"Sit over there," she commanded, pointing to an ancient, but comfortable-looking love-seat. I did as she instructed, but quickly leapt to my feet again as some of the internal springs that had broken through the padding and the surface fabric, tore through the seat of my trousers. I moved over to an open deck-chair in the corner, and reached for her to join me.

"Just relax for a minute," she said softly. Then, standing before me as pale moonbeams streamed through the back window, she doffed her light evening jacket and began to undo the buttons of her silk blouse. Slowly, she opened the flimsy garment and, peeling it from her lovely shoulders, she tossed it aside. She paused, her expression changing to a small tentative smile as she reached behind herself to release the clasp of her pink lace bra. Tossing that garment, too, across the room, she smiled shyly.

"You like?"

The beauty of her finely molded breasts as the moonlight played upon them, made it difficult for me to get the words out. "Verna, you're wonderful," I breathed.

I drank in the vision before me as she turned a full circle in the moonlight. A few moments later, facing me once more, she reached behind her waist again and, opening the zipper of her light tweed skirt, she allowed the garment to slide down over her hips to the floor.

"I just want you to see what you've opted to spend your life with," she said, as pale rays of moonlight rippled over her long shapely legs.

As I watched, entranced, she turned another full circle, clad only in lace panties and silk stockings.

"That's all for tonight," she whispered as I reached for her hand again, but as I pulled her gently toward me, she did not resist. I eased her down into my waiting arms.

Those who have ever attempted to make love in a deck-chair will understand that the next precious hour of alternating, and sometimes mingling, moments of pain and pleasure, left each of us with an unaccustomed readiness for a good night's sleep in our own homes and beds.

I could not imagine a more memorable betrothal evening.

EIGHT

World War

England

Soon, dark times were upon us. Hitler invaded Poland and on that fateful Sunday in September 1939, we heard Prime Minister Neville Chamberlain announce that our country was at war with Germany. I volunteered for flying duties in the RAF, and after a few months waiting around, I finally received instructions to report for kitting out and training. Induction into the service took place at Cardington in the north east of England, and after the selection process, during which one learned what training one would be receiving, we were all instructed to return to our homes and await posting to a Fitness Training Center.

Against my heartfelt preference, I was categorized as a navigator bomb-aimer, and within a few weeks thereafter, I reported for duty at the RAF Bexhill I.T.C. (Initial Training Center), headquartered in a series of hotels on the southern shores near Southampton. The training, almost entirely devoted to parade drills and cross-country running, toned our bodies and our muscles to levels of physical excellence that few of us had ever previously achieved.

We marched and marched and marched, singing whatever bawdy songs our creative members could dream up.

"Left . . . right, left right left . . .
Left, right, left right left . . .
Oooh,
She's got eyes of blue,
and they are a lovely hue.
She's got eyes of blue,
and that's my weakness now.
Oooh,
She's got curly hair,
underneath her underwear,
I didn't know 'til I got there,
but that's my weakness now.
Oooh . . .
Left, right, left right left . . ."

By that time, I'd acquired a Vauxhall saloon car, and was using it to drive back and forth between Coventry and the various RAF stations that were my temporary homes during the months that followed. The sedate and trustworthy car enabled me to come home for weekends whenever permitted, but despite this there were sometimes long intervals between the times that Verna and I were able to see each other.

Since Bessie and Norris had already made plans to marry within the next few months, we'd decided that a double wedding would be a great idea, and from the expense point of view, the economies involved in planning a single wedding reception for two daughters instead of one, would be welcomed by all concerned. It so happened that the approximate date planned for Bessie and Norris's wedding coincided with completion of my flying training at the Bombing and Gunnery School at Evanton in Scotland, and since I'd learned that I would then be posted overseas, it was agreed that that time frame would be optimum for everybody. Military personnel were invariably given a few days leave of absence immediately prior to overseas posting, so a firm date was set. In the weeks and months that followed, Verna kept me posted by letter and by telephone on progress with the wedding and on all the associated arrangements; and with the quite long list of invitations to friends, family and co-workers. Priding themselves on their dress-making abilities, the brides-to-be and their siblings then set about the creation of wedding gowns and the trousseaux for both brides.

Meanwhile Eric, worldly wise and popular, had been counseling me. He'd been like a big brother to me from the day we'd met at the Bexhill-On-Sea RAF Physical Training Station. It was the practice in aircrew training to keep groups of trainees together so that, at the end of each phase of instruction, we would all be posted together to the station where we would complete the next segment. In this manner we'd develop friendships and a camaraderie that would sustain us when the time came for transfer to active duty.

I had come to confide in Eric, and eventually I'd told him of my plans to marry Verna when our training was over. He hadn't commented much on this at first, but as our training neared completion at the Evanton Bombing and Gunnery School in Scotland, he began to express his concern that I was rushing into marriage because of wartime considerations only.

"Nothing will be lost by postponing the event 'til the war is over, Turner," he said. "Right now, you're acting on impulse; you're just not thinking long term."

"But everyone's expecting me to go home at the end of this course, Crut. I can't call it off at this stage in the game. It's just too bloody late. Besides, I wouldn't only be letting Verna down; it would be the whole bloody family. We've got a double wedding planned with her sister, Bessie, and her fiancée. If I let them all down now, Verna will never speak to me again. I just can't do it."

Eric didn't respond to that. Instead, he persuaded other older members of our group to counsel me and warn me of the foolishness of marrying and then immediately departing for war service. It would place more responsibilities on my shoulders at a time when I needed to be unencumbered, they said; and it would be unfair to my intended bride to marry her at this time, perhaps get her pregnant, then leave her with the responsibility of looking after a young child alone. I was assured that later Verna would be glad we'd waited, and once we were off to do our duty, I would be glad, too.

Eventually, I began to wonder about this persistent doctrine. Did they have a point? Were we just being young and foolish in going ahead with the marriage? Were these older ones right about their predictions? Eric and the others did seem to have good reasoning on their side. What if I went home wounded and Verna had to take care of me as well as a child? What if I didn't survive the war and she had a child to rear without a husband? She would marry someone else of course, but the child would be a serious handicap.

And what about me? I didn't even have a career started yet, or even the beginnings of a direction for my life. If I survived the war I would need all my time and energy to do something about that. To have a child as well as a wife to think of at the same time did seem a bit like putting the cart before the horse. In the end, since my own past was littered with snap decisions and impetuous actions, mostly with unhappy consequences, I concluded that Eric and his mature cohorts must be right, and that in their wisdom they were doing their best to save both Verna and me from making a very serious mistake. But the prospect of discussing the matter with Verna proved too daunting for me. Given all the preparations that the whole family had made for the happy occasion, I couldn't think of any way I could broach the matter with her. I went over the scenario in my mind— 'Verna my darling, I've been thinking about the disadvantages and the folly of rushing into marriage right now, and perhaps leaving you with a child to take care of without my help . . .' No, that just wouldn't fly. The whole family would hit the roof and I would lose her forever.

I wrestled with the problem through a number of sleepless nights until I couldn't put it off any longer. In the end I concluded that a reason that would take the matter completely out of our hands and make any discussion academic, would be less difficult for Verna to accept and to live with. Like most of us, the Ogleby family didn't have a home telephone, so I called her at work. I knew she usually brought her lunch with her and ate right there in the packing department, so I called that number shortly after noon. She picked up on the second ring.

"Hello my darling. You know who this is, don't you?"

"Oh I'm so glad you called, Howard," she said. "We only have a few days left before the big day and I wanted to make sure we haven't left anyone off the guest list who should be there. I'm pretty sure we're OK on the Ogleby side, but I just want to go over your own list with you to make sure there aren't any last-minute names you'd like to add."

I swallowed hard, wondering how to start. A pause, then she spoke again.

"Darling? Are you still there?"

"Yes my darling Verna, I'm still here and there's something I have to tell you."

The sudden alarm in her voice reached me loud and clear as she replied.

"What is it, Howard? You sound as if the end of the world has come."

"Well, in a way, it has."

"What is it my darling? Please don't say we have to postpone the wedding this late."

"It's worse than that, Verna. We have to call it off. Home leave has been cancelled for everybody and we have to go straight to the ship from here."

It was a lie that would haunt me for the rest of my life.

I could hear the gasp, and see the incredulity in her face, almost as clearly as if I were in the stockroom with her. After a while she spoke again, her voice hardly above a whisper.

"How could that possibly be, Howard? Everyone gets leave at the end of their training courses."

"I know it's the standard thing my darling, but things overseas are heating up and I suppose they just can't wait to get more reinforcements out there." I said. "I love you my darling Verna and I'll write to you as soon as I can. Tell everybody I'm so desperately sorry, my love."

"I . . . I just don't know what to say, Howard."

I heard her sobs, shallow spasms at first, then deep and hollow. The line went dead.

It was not until we were already aboard ship and making our way slowly out of the Liverpool harbor into the fathomless mists of that October afternoon that the significance of what I'd done gradually dawned on me. I was leaving behind everyone and everything I cared about in the world. I had lied to Verna. I'd broken my promise to her and robbed us both of precious hours together, hours that would have helped strengthen both of us during the long and tumultuous times ahead; hours that we might never be able to replace.

I stood against the rails on deck at the stern of the ship and looked back at the receding gray shores of my homeland. I remained there peering intently in that direction until long after there was anything left to see.

In the days that followed, I immersed myself in the many activities aboard ship; the drills, the physical fitness programs, the navigation and gunnery classes, and briefings on the distant lands that were soon to be our bases of operation. In the evenings I turned for solace to the plentiful supply of liquor that was readily available to aircrew personnel. I tried to console myself with the thought that Verna was probably better off without me.

Life on board for aircrew personnel was relaxed and relatively undisciplined. As the days turned into weeks, the days grew warmer, the night air clear and balmy. We took advantage of every opportunity to bask in the sun and the fresh air, and to prepare for the new life ahead. As the second week began, we were already in the tropics and we were able to take our blankets and sleep on deck. It was an unforgettable experience. In the quiet of the night, the stars hung down as if they were ready to be plucked like ripe fruit. At the sides and at the rear of the ship, luminescent wave-caps kept the seas bright and magical, and in this wonderland, breathing fresh clean air by day and by night, we gathered strength.

By morning of the eleventh day we docked at Freetown in Sierra Leone for re-fueling and reprovisioning, but for reasons that we were not privy to, we were not permitted ashore. We spent two hot, sultry nights tied up at the pier and were all thankful when by noon of the third day we were steaming out into the open sea once more. By late afternoon of the day after that, we were celebrating our crossing of the equator by getting thoroughly drunk. To top off the revelry, Sergeant Derek Hitchcock made his way to the main deck, opened one of the starboard guard-rail gates and walked off the ship. An alert deckhand had the presence of mind to throw him a lifebuoy, but the chances of him being able to reach it seemed slim indeed.

The captain of our ship learned of the mishap almost immediately. He sympathized and hoped we would understand that there was very little he could do about it. Even if he turned the great ship around and tracked back, there was no way that anyone would be able to locate the hapless airman even if he had not already drowned. Furthermore, any such delay and maneuvering would simply increase our exposure to the U-boat threat, and that would further jeopardize the safety of all aboard.

He sighed. "Certainly I've sent signals to all nearby stations and authorities that might conceivably be of help, but frankly, I wouldn't hold out much hope for him." He shook his head. "I'm truly sorry your celebration should end in this way."

His Majesty's submarine HMS Merryweather had been patrolling for most of the day, having taken over watch-dog duty from its predecessor at eight hundred hours. The nation's most valuable cargo was carried by troopships such as the ones the sub was now engaged in helping to protect from the U-boats known to be prowling the area. At seventeen hundred hours, the sub was holding position about twenty yards from one of the big ships' hulls and Sean Hargreaves of the Royal Navy had welcomed his captain's order to surface so as to charge their batteries for a while. It was his turn to serve as 'look-out man' and get some fresh air. When they'd surfaced, he climbed the steps to top-side and took great gulps of the fresh early-evening air. He looked admiringly at each of the massive ships in the convoy that they'd been ordered to protect, and in some ways he envied their crews' opportunities to revel in such spacious quarters and their exposure to nature's elements. He stretched his long limbs and took a few more deep breaths, still peering at the deck of the ship in front of him. Apart from that one chap at the rails, there weren't many souls up there.

Sean stared at that sole figure that seemed to be rocking on uncertain legs and feet. Then as he watched, the man unlatched the heavy rail-gate and began to wrestle with it. Moments later as Sean continued to stare open-mouthed, the lurching figure hauled the gate open and walked straight out into space. Sean's eyes locked onto the tumbling form until it hit the water. Then he heard a second lighter splash as someone tossed a lifebuoy after the jumper. Snapping out of his short-lived trance, he grabbed his speaking tube and yelled for rescue action.

We moped for the rest of the evening, our spirits thoroughly dampened, but when, in the glow of early dawn, the vibration of the ship's turbines became still, and our forward speed slackened, we became curious. Feeling the change in the ship's motion, I leaped out of bed, pulled on my khaki shorts and ran up to the open deck to join others at the starboard rails. Less than twenty yards away, the outline of a submarine's conning tower and the smooth top of its hull were silhouetted against the lightening western sky.

While the sub sat serenely on the surface of the gently rolling ocean swell, someone was being helped onto a small, raft-like conveyance. Shortly thereafter, willing hands returned Derek Hitchcock to the deck that he had so unceremoniously left behind a matter of hours before.

Later that evening when we celebrated his miraculous rescue, Derek told us how it had all been possible. It wasn't so much the skill and speed with which he had been pulled out of the water that had amazed him, though that in itself had been impressive enough; it was the incredible and lucky coincidence that the sub had been sitting on the surface only a few yards away from him at the time, and that its look-out man had actually witnessed his headlong plunge into the brine. He shook his head in wonderment as he relived those fateful moments.

"If it hadn't actually happened to me, I would never have believed such an improbable story," he said.

Regardless of his assurances that he would not push his luck again in such a spectacular manner, we kept a protective eye on Derek, making sure he had company whenever he showed an interest in taking a walk for some fresh air. In truth however, no similar excesses were noted that evening or at any subsequent time in the course of that memorable voyage (Map 2).

In the following days, the seas began to swell a little more and the breezes became somewhat more temperate, still very warm but less oppressive. We became restless, wondering when we might see land again, and whether, the next time we docked for supplies, we would be permitted to go ashore. The senior officers sensed our restlessness, and disciplinary measures and deck drills were resumed. Routine inspections were increased in frequency and thoroughness. We became once more a military body, preparing ourselves for the challenges ahead.

Some ten or twelve days later, as I awoke to sounds of excitement, I felt the great ship turning. I leapt out of my bunk and ran to the nearest porthole. As I peered through the thick glass I could see the sparkling shores of the Bay of Cape Town swinging slowly into view—an unforgettable and breathtaking sight, a panorama of great beauty with the sprawling port of Cape Town nestling into the base of Table Mountain which rose majestically behind it and spread out to a broad and flattened top in the background.

The news traveled like wildfire. We were going ashore! The ship would be in dock for at least a full day to refuel and re-provision, and we would be allowed on shore for the whole of that time. We scrambled as fast as we could to polish our boots and our buttons. We rushed to the showers and the wash basins to spruce ourselves up for the great adventure to come; we rushed through our breakfasts so that we could be on our way before the mad dash that was bound to follow the early birds. There was, however, one small hitch. We were not yet in port.

For the next long hour we found ourselves cursing our unbearably slow progress as the great ship made its way across the lapping waters of the bay toward that colorful oasis whose glistening shores now spread languorously across the whole of our horizon. And for most of that hour I stood against the rails on deck, gazing at the approaching sun-splashed houses and the busy city streets, alive with men, women and children going about their work and play, and I thought of the girl I'd left behind and all that might have been.

I do not know what Cape Town is like today, but in those early days of World War II it was a colorful and attractive metropolis, bustling with people and activity. My friend Johnny Johnson had come ashore with me and we were already window-shopping along the main thoroughfare. We saw merchandise of excellent quality and little evidence of wartime shortages. After diving into an Italian ice-cream shop for a taste of the multi-colored extravagances offered by that establishment, we stepped off the sidewalk to take a look at whatever was on the other side of the street. We didn't get far, for a fast moving, fine looking car bore down on us and screeched to a halt about a foot from where we were standing. A well-set mature man with receding dark hair bounded out of the driver's side and strode toward us, extending his hand in greeting and in apology for almost knocking us down.

"I'm Fred Stemmet," he said "and to atone for my carelessness, my wife and I would like you to have dinner with us this evening. First, however, would you please get in the car so that we can take you on a tour of the city and its surroundings?" I gaped in disbelief at this affable stranger. I looked at Johnny, as if expecting him to explain this extraordinary encounter, but Johnny, too, seemed as bewildered as I. "Thank you very much," I mumbled, and before we'd had time to gather our wits again, we found ourselves comfortably settled in the back of Fred Stemmet's car. Later, we would come to realize that our impromptu meeting with Fred and Elaine Stemmet would prove one of the most fortunate encounters that either of us would experience during the whole of our Middle-East tour of duty.

After showing us around the major shops and restaurants, Fred and Elaine took us by cable-car to the top of Table Mountain, and from there we explored the huge area of grape-growing country known as Constantia Valley. This, we were told, was a vital wine-making area for Cape Town, and we would taste the finished product later at lunch. 'Later' proved to be around 2 pm when the Stemmets drove us back to their home for that occasion. We sat around a polished rosewood table, drinking the promised wines and relaxing in a large, cool and uncluttered living-dining room, where colorful rugs were scattered over a waxed and polished teak floor, and an enormous ceiling fan with blades woven from some sort of basket-making material, left one with an overall impression of airiness and good taste.

In the course of a lunch consisting of an unusual combination of cold-cuts and exotic fruits, Elaine continued to quiz Johnny and me about our likes and dislikes.

"I don't know whether you fellows smoke," she said, but we've learned from some of the men and women who have preceded you, that the only cigarettes you can get in the Middle-East war zones are Woodbines and some terrible local brand called Victory Vees. If you like, we can do something about that."

"Well, I don't know about Johnny, but I'm not much of a smoker Elaine," I replied. "Still, an occasional cigarette after eating or with a glass of Ale, does help one relax."

Johnny, normally quite reticent, responded more enthusiastically. "Nothing would be more welcome for me than a few good cigarettes from time to time. When I've had a really tough day, I'm apt to chain-smoke in the evening to get over it."

"Well, that's good to know," Elaine said, "We'll see that you get some Players or Craven 'A's, or some Goldflakes from time to time, to make you feel at home."

After lunch, more sight-seeing until the daylight had turned to dusk, and from dusk to the brightly-lit sparkle of the Cape Town evening. Time for dinner.

The French restaurant to which the Stemmets drove us for the evening meal was memorable, not only for its delicious cuisine which would have rivaled anything in pre-war London, but also for its decor. At first, I assumed that the restaurant had no roof, that it was open to the skies, for when I looked up I was able to see a bright crescent moon reclining in a deep blue, star-studded sky. It was picture perfect but as our hosts later explained, it was, indeed, a picture. Somehow the architects of the illusion had created a cleverly lit, three-dimensional display to delight the clientele in general and the romantically inclined in particular. It was in any case a luxurious and relaxing environment for our evening with Fred and Elaine, and Johnny and I savored every minute of it.

As dinner progressed, Elaine, petite, vivacious and friendly began to question us about our families and about some of the other things we might be short of and would most need in the course of our Middle-East service, things that our families might not be able to send in sufficient quantities, if at all.

"I wonder whether you fellows would care for things like dark fruit cakes and Chiver's or Robinson's marmalade, or canned fruit and meats, socks and sweaters." We listened intently as it became clear that Elaine was planning to send us these things, both necessities and luxuries, and we assured her that we would be most grateful for whatever she cared to send, whenever she might find the time and opportunity to send it.

"Well," she said, brushing a swathe of auburn hair from her smiling face, "Now that we've got that settled, let's make a note of your military addresses and birthdays, and your preferences in food and clothing."

This charming couple's generosity went even further. They questioned us on the latest shortages in our homeland and asked for our home addresses so that Elaine could occasionally send parcels of things or foods that our families were missing the most and could no longer obtain. It was all part of their contribution to the war effort, Elaine assured us, and they were both thankful that they were in a position to do their part in this way. If we were risking our lives, they said, it was up to them to help us in any way they could while we were taking those risks.

Elaine and Fred, it seemed, had decided to 'adopt' Johnny and me as they had already adopted many other servicemen and women who'd been fortunate enough to meet them on their way to their overseas destinations. In the course of time we would discover just how sincere their decision had been. Already we had, by a benign stroke of fortune, found new friends and enjoyed an unforgettable time in this metropolitan paradise. By the time the evening was over, we were planning post-war exchange visits to each other's homes, but before we'd had time to reflect at length on the delightful outcome of our visit to Cape Town, our stay had run its course.

We said our good-byes to Elaine and Fred, and shortly thereafter, our huge floating headquarters carried us quietly away from the quayside into the darkness of Table Bay.

NINE

April 1941

The evacuation of Greece

The rumored posting of the entire squadron turned out to be real. On April 12th the mess notice board carried the information. Squadron Leader Pike had taken over from Wing-commander D. C. Smith as Squadron Commander, and he would be flying north a day ahead of the rest of us to prepare for our arrival at Kabrit in the Nile delta. Before leaving, we were to muster the following morning for a crew-call to review changes and learn which navigators and air-gunners would be flying with which pilots for the flight to Port Sudan, and then onward to Kabrit.

Since S\Ldr Pike had been appointed squadron commander, he'd taken over part of Wing-Commander Smith's crew, which meant that I would be flying with someone else. Geordie (A.C. Cox) had stayed with him. There were some other changes as well, and the final line-up would be called out on the parade ground and the appropriate officers and NCOs asked to step forward as each man heard his name called.

A clear morning greeted us on April 13th as we took our places on the parade ground. Wing Commander Smith praised the work we'd done in protecting our precious convoys and in striking so effectively at the enemy. Then he handed over to Squadron Leader pike.

"Please step forward and each crew stand in a separate group as I call your names," Pike began.

"After we've completed the crew-call, we shall disperse and stand-by for announcements of take-off times for Port Sudan, and then on to Kabrit."

Then he began the call:

"Squadron Leader Gethin."

Gethin was first to be named on account of the fact that he'd just won the Distinguished Flying Cross, and had been promoted.

"Sgt.Harding, Sgt. Neale, LAC Shearer."

All four stepped forward and stood together as their names were called.

"Pilot Officer Wilson, Sgt. Zeiting, Sgt.Holbrook, LAC Hutton."

In their turn, they stepped forward.

"F/ Lt. Scott, Sgt. Cruttenden, Sgt. Bushell, LAC. Morrison."

"Pilot Officer Tremlett, Sgt. Layton, Sgt. Thynne."

And so it went as Pike named each man in each crew in his lengthy list.

I glanced at each one of these stalwarts as crew by crew they stepped forward.

I was glad that we were going to stay together. We were going into another war zone, probably more perilous than the one we were leaving, but we were a coordinated group now; we were a team, better able to support each other as the need would be upon us. Yes, I was glad that those in command had organized things this way. My chest heaved.

Within a week, we were on our way north, refueling at Port Sudan, and within minutes of landing at Kabrit, we learned that we would be leaving for Heraklion on the Island of Crete the next day. We would get our further briefings upon arrival.

The following morning, five of our nine aircraft took off at 1100 hrs, and the remaining crews were briefed to follow us at about the same time the next day.

No sooner had we landed at the Heraklion airfield in Crete, and fueled up ready for the next day's flying, than we got our briefings. We would be taking part in the evacuation of Greece, escorting the convoys to safety (Map 3).

On the 25th, we took to the skies to find the evacuation convoys and protect them from enemy aircraft. I was crewed with S/Ldr Scott and air-gunner Sgt. Bushell.

The melee that ensued was almost comical. We eventually found the convoy somewhat west of the expected position, making its way southbound from the island of Hydra to Suda Bay. Simultaneously, a northbound convoy had arrived on the scene and seemed to be having difficulty finding its way past the southbound ships. To add to the confusion, Number 30

Squadron had been briefed to participate in the escort program, too, but neither we nor they had been informed of this plan. Not surprisingly, we arrived on the scene at he same time, and spent the first several minutes chasing each other before the situation became clear.

Also participating in this melee were a host of enemy aircraft. In addition to a considerable number of Junkers 87 dive-bombers, we found ourselves chasing Ju 88s that we had no hope of catching, and defending ships against Messersmitt110s that could easily out-fly us. The only factor in our favor was that the enemy seemed unaware of our performance limitations. When we appeared on the scene, they scattered. Those that stayed discovered that what we lacked in speed we mostly made up for in maneuverability. On balance, our defense of the convoy turned out to be pretty effective.

Three of our Blenheims were at 8, 000 ft when a burst of anti-aircraft fire from one of the ships revealed a dive-bomber commencing an attack. As we then took a line-astern formation, we saw the remainder of the dive bombers following the leader.

We followed them into their dive. Unlike the Blenheim IV, however, the dive-bombers were built with the capability to limit their speed in a dive, whereas we accelerated quickly and were upon them before they realized what was happening. F\Lt Whittall, our number three, flying L9237, got in several bursts at close range. Smoke poured from the aircraft he'd hit, and it fell away. As we got in a series of bursts into one of the JU87s, Whittal zeroed in on another, but he was now among

104

them, taking hits to his own aircraft from the rear. Smoke belched from his starboard engine as he was attempting to pull out of his dive. Another Ju87 got in his sights as his dive continued, and despite his own perilous predicament, Whittal continued to blaze away with his battery of front-mounted Browning guns, managing to put yet another close- range burst into his German Quarry before disappearing in a trail of thick black smoke. I stared after him, knowing that the tenacious and heroic action I'd just witnessed was that fine airman's last, and at that moment I raged inside at the futility of it all, at the waste of human ingenuity and skill; of the countless thousands of mothers sacrificing the bounty of their wombs to the mindless slaughter, and of the fathers on both sides mourning the loss of their sons; of the endless destruction of the treasures of the ages, and again the futility. I knew only that I was overwhelmed by it all, that my eyes were brimming with unshed tears, and that as we continued to dive I was bursting with anger and despair.

We were not able to assess the extent of damage to the enemy, nor even make a useful guess at how many of them failed to make it back to their base, but we had at least succeeded in our basic mission—to protect the convoy. Our aircraft were not able to catch up with any of the enemy as they scattered for home, but it was gratifying to see that they were still carrying their bombs when they fled. By 1130 hrs, the skies around the convoy had been cleared of enemy aircraft.

We set course and, one after another, our battered machines limped home to our base at the Heraklion airfield. Whittal's L9237 was not among them.

The following day with seven aircraft serviceable, we set out to rendezvous with another convoy but could not find it. In the end we were obliged to return to base for refueling. We eventually located the convoy some twelve miles northwest of Suda Bay and escorted it into Suda. When we landed, we learned that F/Lt Corbould had flown to Melame to get a new fuel tank to replace his damaged one, and had returned with King George of the Hellenes and Crown Prince Paul on board. What next?

On April 28th, the last day of the evacuation, three of our aircrews, including my own, were ordered to intercept a large naval convoy west of Melos. On the day itself, scanning the horizon through the mists of that April morning, we eventually sighted the host of ships just after 7 am. Taking up formation in nose-to-tail line astern, we began our spiral descent to rendezvous astern of the rear cruiser in accordance with the planned and agreed procedure. Maps and charts flew everywhere as we began the dive, and in my preoccupation with the task of keeping them out of the captain's line of vision, I hardly noticed the train of staccato sounds beginning to drown out the engine noise.

As I finally grasped what was happening, I glanced to my right and stared in disbelief as a series of small jagged holes spread themselves across our starboard wing.

I tore my eyes away and turned to the captain.

"Christ! They're shooting at us. Our own bloody Navy is trying to shoot us down!"

The captain nodded but continued to concentrate on the now more demanding task of following the leader as he modified his downward spiral plunge to include evasive action. The cruiser's gunfire continued to rake our formation. It persisted even as we took up our prearranged positions a couple of hundred feet above the water and about a half-mile aft of the rearmost cruiser. The trigger-happy gunner was still firing at us even as we maneuvered into position and identified ourselves as friendly aircraft by lowering our undercarriages, and by firing green cartridges. The pounding went on for many more terrifying minutes before the cruiser's gunner realized what we were there for.

No serious damage to our peppered aircraft was evident at first, but when the firing had ceased, we could see that L9044's starboard engine was smoking. A few minutes later, it caught fire. Wagging his wings to signal his departure, Paul Gordon-Hall peeled off and set course for base, flying on his port engine only, and streaming black smoke as his aircraft eventually disappeared in the distance. We turned our attention once more to our escort duties.

The mists had evaporated by the time we'd returned and touched down at the Heraklion airfield. Bright sunlight reflected off the row of aircraft canopies as we taxied past the line-up on the ramp. I looked for L9044, but did not see it. If they'd managed to stay aloft, they would certainly have landed by this time. There was no other answer. They'd gone down.

I followed Mike Bushell and our captain, S/Ldr Scott into the operations hut for de-briefing by acting squadron commander, F/Lt Corbould. A mood of futility and frustration prevailed as Sq/Ldr Gethin described the events of the morning.

"Just how will the Service go about telling all the relatives of that crew, that their loved ones have been shot out of the sky by the very people they risked their lives to protect?" he said.

Corbould seemed puzzled. "Who are you talking about?" he said.

"Gordon-Hall and his chaps, of course," Gethin replied.

"Those fellows have already turned up," Corbould said. "And I can assure you, they are very much alive."

The mood brightened immediately and everyone spoke at once.

"Where's his aircraft? We didn't see it on the field."

"How did they get here, then?"

"When we didn't see his number out there, we assumed they'd gone down."

Corbould raised his arms for quiet.

"If you'll just take a look in the Mess hut, you'll see the three of them catching up on their breakfast," he said. "And I'm sure they'll be glad to give you the 'pucka gen' themselves."

F\Lt Gordon-Hall greeted us as we joined them at the long bare-topped wooden table in the air-crew Mess hut. He had a fairly ugly scratch along the length of his left cheek, but otherwise seemed in good shape.

"What took you so long?" he said. "Couldn't you chaps bear to leave those friendly convoys?"

Again, we all began firing questions at the same time.

"Where's your aircraft?"

"How d'you get here?"

Gordon-Hall stopped us short.

"Tell you what," he said. "Oultram is the chap to fill you in, and he's just about finished his sausage and mash. What about it, Sergeant?"

Oultram, still with his mouth full, nodded. I noted that he had a large, angry looking bruise on his forehead.

"We were just very lucky," he said when he'd swallowed the last of his food.

"I can tell you that it's not that easy to get out of a gun turret when you're under water. Anyway, that's the way it was. When the airplane hit the water, the nose went under and the cockpit followed in a few seconds. Then the gun turret went under after that. I can remember looking forward as the wings hit, and I was mesmerized. It could have been easier but I just didn't react fast enough. The problem was that I couldn't get out of the top. I had to pull myself out from below and crawl forward through the fuselage to get out through the pilot's top canopy." He paused.

"The gun turret didn't jettison, you see, so there was no other way unless I had had an axe, and could have smashed the bloody thing." He paused again, trying to recall the sequence of events.

"In a way, it was probably a good thing because as I went down below, I saw the dinghy and I realized that I had to get that out, too. So I unhitched that from its stowage ring and dragged it along through the fuselage, then tossed it out of the pilot's top canopy." He paused again, marshalling his thoughts.

"Of course, that's when I saw that the captain was in trouble, and Sgt. Poole was still struggling to get himself loose from behind the navigation table. It was a good thing he got himself free seconds after I reached the cockpit, because there was no way I could have helped both him and the captain at the same time."

"Anyway, the two of us then struggled together to get the captain's seat buckle undone. You know, it's just amazing how difficult simple things become when you can't actually see what you're doing. It's not that the water wasn't clear, it's just that it was all stirred up because of all of our frantic efforts and we were just milling around in a sea of bubbles. Of course the additional problem was the urgency. The captain couldn't breathe. He was going to drown if we didn't get him loose fast. Finally the buckle let go."

Another pause as Oultram continued to relive the experience.

"Between us we were able to drag the captain out of his seat and out through the top exit, onto the port wing." He shook his head from side to side as he recalled the struggle. Then he grabbed his tea mug and took a couple of swallows.

"And pretty soon after that, we managed to haul ourselves and the captain aboard the dinghy."

There was quiet for a while as each one of us, in his own way, seemed to be trying to imagine the experience for himself, putting himself in the same situation, wondering how he would have reacted—and whether he would have measured up.

In a few moments, Oultram took up his account again.

"Then we set about paddling toward the shore a couple of miles distant, but soon after we'd got started, we were amazed to see that we had company. Someone else was in the water, someone swimming some yards ahead of us who also seemed to be swimming for the same shore. The stranger turned and saw us, then he yelled at us in Greek. When he saw that we were not able to understand what he was saying, he unhitched a coil of rope from his belt. Then he tied one end to a boot which, as far as I could see, had also been hitched to his belt, and without further comment, hurled it at us. Treading water until he could see that the boot had reached its target and that the rope had been secured to the dinghy, the stranger turned and, after tying the other end of the rope around his waist he began swimming again, towing the dinghy behind him as the three of us continued to paddle ourselves along." He took a breath.

"When we finally got to the shore and were able to take a good look at his drenched uniform, we could see that he was a Greek soldier, evidently making his own separate bid to escape the Nazis. We could see that he was large and very well muscled, so it wasn't difficult to understand how his help had made a difference to our progress.

We thanked him, of course, but when we tried to persuade him to come with us to our base, he held up both his hands in a gesture that made it clear that this was not at all what he wanted to do. In a jiffy, the bloke was gone."

The adjutant joined us, tea-mug in hand.

"Better get some rest, chaps. It's back to Kabrit for the lot of us in the morning, and we've got to take absolutely everything with us."

And so it was. By mid-day of May 1st, Crete and the evacuation project, and our encounters with our trigger-happy brothers in arms, were history.

The author (foreground) taking a break on Lake Timsah, Egypt, with Eric (Crut) Cruttenden, sans moustache,

TEN

Kenya, January 1942

"Gentlemen," I said, "you may never need the astronavigation skills that you learned in your courses in Australia, and that I am now refreshing for you—but if you ever do, you will thank your stars (pun intended) that in the short weeks that you were here, you listened and practiced with all the concentration you were able to muster.

When you leave here, you will go north to an air-crew pool in the El Alamein area, and quickly thereafter, you will be posted to a squadron. Once there, you will be assigned to a crew and the guidance of your aircraft to the target and safely home again after your appointed missions, will be entirely your responsibility."

A crew-cropped, serious looking airman in the front row raised his hand.

"What if the sky is obscured, either by cloud-cover or mist?"

"Well, if it's day time and you're over the water, you reel out a little gadget we call a tail-drift-sight. That's a brightly colored object like a small kite, and it flies there on the end of the long string you've played out from the rear of the aircraft. As you watch the tail, and note which side of the aircraft it flies, and the approximate amount of the 'drift' in degrees, you then know how much you have to correct your course for wind-drift."

Another question came to me from a burly sergeant in the back row.

"What if it's a totally black night and you can't see a thing."

"Good question, but it's one the Operations Officers have to address. It's up to them to determine what weather is flyable and what is not. The general idea is that although we want to strike the enemy as often and as hard as possible, that has to be weighed against the high desirability of getting our aircraft and crews back home again after the raid so that they can strike again another day."

"If the mission is vital and maximum risks must be taken, you place your faith in 'dead-reckoning' and fly the course according to the maps and charts you have available, and the prevailing-wind information that you will have obtained from the briefing officer." I paused.

"In any case, it's worth knowing that totally black nights are rare. Even what seems black at first, turns out to be more navigable as your eyes become accustomed to the darkness. It's amazing what you can see after twenty minutes in the gloom—even without all those carrots the fighter pilots are told to gorge on."

"It's a rare occasion that you can't see the breakers as you approach the shoreline after a mission across the Med. You can see the white foam tops breaking along the coast, and they clearly reveal the shape of the coastline. From that you can pin-point your position and calculate the correction you have to make to get back on course."

I scanned the sea of earnest faces. "Any more questions?" I asked.

No one answered. They seemed to have had enough for that particular session.

"See you again at 1400 hours tomorrow."

I watched them stepping down from the tiered rows of benches, filing past my table, smart and orderly, in contrast with the not quite so disciplined appearance of their devil-may-care brothers in the Australian Army, and I wondered how, at the tender age of twenty-three, I had come to be teaching anything to anyone.

My unexpected posting had happened quite suddenly. When our entire squadron had returned to Kabrit from Heraklion, only six usable aircraft remained. These were allocated to the most experienced pilots and aircrews who were then ordered to proceed east to Lydda and work from that base to do battle with El Raschid, a rebel intent upon waging a war of his own and bent on destroying the Iraqi oil pipe line.

From the remainder of the available air crew members, two pilot officers, one commissioned navigator and one flight-sergeant navigator (myself), were assigned to fill vacancies for instructors at the RAF Pre-Operations Training School at Nakuru, Kenya. I didn't learn where the rest of 203 Squadron's air-crews were posted, but I assumed they'd been sent to join the Army's close-support forces in the Western Desert.

The squadron adjutant advised me that the twenty-two hundred mile journey to Nakuru would be spread over two and a half days with breaks at Khartoum and Entebbe, Uganda. We would be taken as far as Entebbe in a Short Sunderland Flying Boat which would make the flight in two separate six hour legs on two separate days. Then, after another overnight break at Entebbe, a Blenheim IV would pick up those of us bound for Nakuru.

Within forty-eight hours I was on my way. The other three were due to follow a week later.

The big bird lumbered across the broad expanse of the waters of the Nile estuary, gathering speed and riding more smoothly as the seconds ticked by. Soon its huge hull broke the surface and we were free and flying toward the infinite desert, the rippling haze, and the rising sun. As we gained altitude, our starboard wing dipped, signaling our turn to a southerly course. Through the haze I could see the river as we lined up to follow it into Upper Egypt and the African hinterland beyond. The stinging sand and oppressive heat were gone now. Clean cool air filled my lungs as I breathed deeply and relaxed in my seat. I looked around at the other passengers, nearly all in RAF and Army uniforms. Some, like me I supposed, were on their way to postings in Kenya, but when we landed at Entebbe on the shores of Lake

Victoria, there would be a parting of the ways and other aircraft would take us on to our several and separate destinations.

I turned my attention to the landscape below, and watched as vast expanses of sand and scrub came into hazy view and slid slowly under our wings. For the first hour at least, the river was always in sight, sometimes to the left and sometimes to the right, and here and there, clusters of low buildings, some pink, some white, mostly near the river banks, gave evidence of continued habitation.

I looked around the cabin again. In the opposite aisle seat, a well built, sandy-haired NCO in the dark blue uniform of the RAAF (Royal Australian Air Force), noticed my glance in his direction. He looked right at me with clear hazel eyes. "Where you headed, mate?" he asked in that unmistakable, half-Cockney accent.

"I've got a notion that I'm headed for the same place as you." I replied. "I'm on my way to Nakuru in Kenya, where I'm supposed to be giving pre-operational instruction to Australian aircrews."

"You're right on, mate." He replied with a lop-sided grin. "Looks like I'm going to be one of your students. Anyhow," he said, sticking out a large brown hand and reaching across the aisle, "My name's Andy Campbell, and I'm right glad to meet you."

"Same here Andy. I'm Howard Layton. Mostly they call me Turner or Buzz. Take your pick. Turner after the famous singer, Turner Leighton, or Buzz after an English town that you've probably never heard of called

Leighton Buzzard. Anyway, glad to meet you, too, Andy." After a pause I went on,

"This instructional posting is supposed to double as a rest period for some of us, but from what I hear from others who've been there, the stint at Nakuru is pretty concentrated, and the flying goes on all day and through much of the night. Reason for that is that the pilots have to hone their night-flying skills as well as their daylight flying, and navigators need a chance to get a bead on some stars and refine their astro-navigation, to get them ready for ops."

"Right on, mate. They told us this is the last stop before the real thing, and I can't wait to get it done."

We continued our chatting across the aisle, and I learned that Andy had been in the service about eighteen months. He'd completed pilot training some three months previously. Thereafter, he and a lot of his class-mates had opted for a Middle East posting, but had stayed in Australia, helping to train other incoming aircrews while awaiting their own turn for pre-op training in North Africa.

The minutes and the hours slid by and I began to learn more about Australians and their attitude toward the war, and more about Andy in particular. I decided that if the Australians I would meet and work with in the course of my stay at Nakuru, would turn out to be anything like Andy, I was in for a congenial and rewarding time.

Outside, the sand and haze of the Egyptian landscape had been left behind. We were flying in clear air and bright sunlight, interrupted only by occasional wisps of white cloud. We drifted and thought our own thoughts. At length, my ears told me that we were beginning our descent into the Khartoum area, as the waters of the Upper Nile rose to greet us.

A unit of His Majesty's army provided us with a hot meal and a bed in comfortable quarters in which large fans and high ceilings rendered the noticeably warmer air less oppressive. Next day, after a hearty English breakfast of sausage and eggs, we were airborne again and on our way by about 9am. In minutes, the roller-coaster ride of the climb-out was behind us, and for the next five hours we flew in smooth clear air, left once more to our reminiscences and our ponderings about the days, weeks and months ahead.

I closed my eyes and drifted. Soon, I slept.

I awoke to the changing pressure in my ears as our flying behemoth began to lose altitude. A sparkling coastline rose to greet us, and soon we were skimming across the crystal waters of Lake Victoria, source of the Nile, nearly 4,000 feet above sea level, just kissing the surface at first, then cutting deeper furrows into the glistening blue-green infinity of Africa's largest lake. As our speed bled off, the pilot turned our aircraft toward the shore, toward the shacks and boardwalks, wooden piers, derricks and warehouses that were the docks of the Port of Entebbe.

An RAF officer in regular blue uniform, rather than khaki shirt and shorts, greeted us as we disembarked. I noted that Andy and I were the only ones to leave the aircraft. The remaining passengers were evidently bound for other destinations.

"Follow me chaps," the officer said. "I'm Flying Officer Dennis Stratfield, and my job is to look after you until we fly you out of here tomorrow morning." He eyed the two of us.

"Two of you for Nakuru, is that right?" We nodded our agreement.

"OK, good. We've got a buggy here for you, to take you to your overnight palatial quarters, so we might as well get on our way."

The buggy turned out to be a sort of oversized Jeep of dubious vintage, but plenty big enough for the two of us bound for Nakuru, and for the driver and our host. We climbed aboard with our kit-bags and settled ourselves as comfortably as possible while Dennis filled us in about arrangements.

"We're putting you up at the local airfield where there's a sort of Nissen-hut dormitory for NCO aircrews. Then, down the road a bit—actually less than a quarter of a mile—there's an aircrew mess where everybody, officers and NCO aircrews, eat." He paused.

"We'll drop you off first at your sleeping quarters so you can unpack and freshen up. Then, if you're too bushed to walk to the mess, there's a jeep that will be coming by at 1800 hours to give you a ride."

"And there's another jeep that'll bring you back if you like." he added.

"Most people welcome the walk and the chance of a bit of exercise, but it's up to you." He studied our faces to see if we'd got it so far. "The Blenheim that will take you to Nakuru, will arrive some time this evening, and transport will pick you up for the flight at 0700 hours tomorrow morning." He looked at each of us in turn, "Any questions?"

We shook our heads. My guess was that both Andy and I were bent on washing up and getting something to eat and we didn't want to prolong the preliminaries. In a few more minutes, we pulled alongside the familiar caterpillar-shaped Nissen-hut structure, our lodging for the night.

"See you later gentlemen," Dennis said cheerily as he pulled out onto the road again. "Look out for the animals; they're not always friendly—especially after dark."

Then he was gone.

ELEVEN

Animals? What was that about?
I followed Andy up the front steps of our billet for
our night at Entebbe. He hauled the screen door open
and I followed him inside. A row of neatly-spaced cots
stretched the length of each side of the interior. Folded
sheets and blankets had been placed on low benches at
the foot of each cot. Aside from the less than rugged
construction of the cots, we could have been in Kabrit or
Heraklion or Aden. I felt quite at home.

"What about it, Andy. Shall we just wash up and go
get some chow, and leave the sorting out 'til later?" I
asked.

"Suits me mate. Let's see what they've got."

The walk to the Mess proved as simple and as short as
Dennis had promised. Telephone poles supporting
electric cables as well as phone lines lined both sides of
the narrow dirt road. Between them, scrub and tropical
bushes with a variety of thickly foliaged trees that didn't
look at all tropical, cropped up here and there, marking
the borders. I was vaguely disappointed that I didn't see
any of the flat-topped Acacias or the Ironwoods that
were supposed to abound in tropical areas. We could
have been strolling along a country road in Europe. In

123

little more than the predicted quarter mile, a bend in the road brought us face to face with a long, single-story, concrete building fronted by a well kept lawn from whose center, an impressive flag-pole rose majestically. Again, the half dozen steps up to the entrance indicated that for their own good reasons, the planners and builders had avoided putting ground floors at ground level.

Inside, the usual long mess tables were absent. Modest sized, solid-looking rectangular tables that looked to be capable of seating about eight persons each were placed randomly through the dining area, filling but not overcrowding it.

On closer inspection I was able to see that the table-tops were actually thick slabs of polished mahogany. I was surprised at first, but then I remembered that some of the world's largest mahogany trees were said to flourish in this part of Uganda. Instead of full-sized tablecloths, large woven raffia squares served as place-mats at each seating place, and also wherever condiments and serving dishes were located.

The sight of all that polished wood brought a welcome touch of elegance to this remote staging post, but there it ended. The inevitable line-up for the standard cafeteria type serving arrangements that prevailed in all the RAF training and operational establishments that I could remember, was repeated here, too. The line stretched from the far end of the room where the serving counter occupied the entire width of the Mess, and ended close to where Andy and I were standing.

Not a crowd, but not the Ritz, either.

Andy and I sat at one of the tables near the serving area and ate our dinners in comparative silence, each lost in his own thoughts.

The food proved more appetizing than I'd expected; lamb and mint-sauce with sweet potatoes and canned peas. Fresh bread that still had that newly baked smell to it was complemented by real farmhouse-type butter, and the fruit pie that followed the main course did credit to its creator.

A tap on my shoulder interrupted my reverie.

"Are you the navigator that's going to Nakuru, Flight-Sergeant?"

A short, thick-set, heavy-featured RAF officer was looking at me almost accusingly from under a pair of bushy light-brown eyebrows.

"Well?"

"Excuse me, uh, yes sir" I replied, gulping down my last piece of pie.

"Well you'd better sit up front tomorrow, even though I know every inch of this territory by heart. You and your Australian companion had better be out there on time. I don't enjoy this taxi service they've got me on, so I want to get it over as quickly as possible. Understood?"

"Yes sir!" I replied

He took a nearby seat on the opposite side of the table, unfurling several flight charts.

"By the way, I'm Flying-Officer Albert Braun," He continued. "And right now, I want to review tomorrow's procedures with you so we'll have less to do in the morning."

Andy looked at me desperately.

"I'm flagging a bit, mate." he said, still toying with his dessert. Then he stood and addressed F\O Braun.

"Sir, I'm feeling pretty bushed, so would it be all right if I go on ahead and get myself a good night's sleep?"

Braun seemed to be considering the request as if Andy had been asking for ten days sick leave.

"You may go if you must," he said.

By the time I left the Mess nearly an hour later, the deep red sunset of the early evening had been replaced by an almost ink-black tropical night, full of the sounds and songs of an awakened animal and insect kingdom. The occasional street lamps were lit now, casting alternate pools of light and shadow across my path as I made my way steadily back. Reversing the walk we'd taken a few hours earlier, I set off around the bend and started up the straight quarter-mile.

After a while, I became aware that something or someone was moving up ahead. At first, it was just a flickering of light reflected from the middle of the road about fifty feet ahead of me. The patches of light grew larger as I seemed to be overtaking it.

Then I knew. As the creature was making its way past one of the street lamps, there was no mistaking the form and the black and yellow spotted coat. I stood there in the shadows, fascinated by the slow loping stride of that graceful animal. I could just make out the rise and fall of its back muscles as the dappled amber hide that stretched over them reflected light from the street lamp. The glistening coat rippled as I stared in wonderment and in a paroxysm of cold fear.

There was no way I could retreat, or do anything useful to help myself in that moment. In the absence of any inspiration that might have helped me, I commenced strolling again like an automaton, the pace the same as before I had become aware that I had company. I was not even conscious of the fact that I was moving—or even breathing.

The leopard turned its head and stared briefly in my direction. Two large yellow eyes seemed to appraise me as friend or foe. I could almost sense that it was deliberating whether to turn around and come closer to investigate—to determine whether I fell into the category of predator or prey. Then, in the next heart-stopping seconds, the sleek head turned away from me again and the animal continued padding along the road with that same steady loping, nose-to-the-ground gait, haunches rising and falling, their image staying with me until the outline of its powerful form eventually merged with the distant dark.

I stopped walking, and for what seemed an eternity, I stood there under the diffuse light of the street lamps, peering into the darkness ahead, straining my eyes to catch any sign of movement. Satisfied that the creature was far enough away, I turned my attention to the task of locating the hut. I forced my legs into motion again. With a thumping heart, and with as much stealth as I could muster, I made my way to the safety of the rough wooden structure and up the steps to the door. As quietly as I could manage, I let myself in.

When the trembling had subsided, and the beating of my heart had slowed, I propped myself up in my bed, writing-paper in hand, and thought about what I would tell Verna about the day's events.

'*I've been posted to an entirely different location, my darling, and there's so much I could tell you about it if only I were free to do so. It's a different climate here, and my job is going to be different from what I've been doing. Actually, I'm still on my way, and perhaps I shall be allowed to tell you more when I arrive. Meanwhile, I expect your letters to me will take a bit longer to get here, and mine to you. So remember that I think of you every day and in the night as well. Verna, I miss you so. I live for the day when you will run toward me again and do that excited little tap-dance with your feet; when I can wrap my arms around you and run my fingers through your chestnut hair.*'

With that thought in mind I drifted into blissful slumber.

The next day looked much better after a good night's sleep and a hearty breakfast. Andy and I were out there at the front of the hut with our kit-bags by our sides, well before the jeep arrived to take us to the airfield. The driver dropped us at the run-up area, where our Blenheim IV aircraft awaited us. I breathed a sigh of relief that we were actually ahead of Flying Officer Braun. Andy and I managed to get ourselves on board and our kit-bags stowed before he arrived on the scene. He was not far behind, however, and as he climbed into the cockpit, I heard him barking at the ground crew chief to remove the tail and wing tie-downs. Then, as he settled into his seat and buckled his seat-belt, he turned to me with his orders.

"I hope you have the course worked out for us, Flight Sergeant," he said.

"I certainly have, sir" I replied, "And since the winds are light this morning, the flight should not be more than an hour and a half. That is, of course, depending on the cruising speed you prefer to use."

He grunted something I wasn't able to decipher.

"Let's get going," he said, and with that, he handed me the pre-flight check-list and proceeded to check and confirm each item as I called it out.

"Gills," I called out.

He grasped the wheel at his right that controlled the series of hinged metal flaps that surrounded the cowling on the two radial engines, and turned it until the gills were fully open. They fanned themselves out at an angle, leaving rectangular spaces for air to enter and flow all around the tops of the cylinders. By this means, cooling for the ground run-up and for taxiing would be suitably enhanced. Next, the flight controls—ailerons, rudder and elevator— were exercised to ensure that they moved smoothly and easily. Mixture and propeller checks followed, and finally, the captain pushed the throttles forward for a routine engine run-up to check the revs-per-minute drop for each magneto in each pair, when he switched its twin off and on again.

As he throttled back after the run-up, he called the ground operations officer for permission to taxi. Then he waved the ground mechanics away, released the brakes, and opened the throttles for taxiing.

No movement.

I could see the bushy brows furrow in puzzlement and irritation. He thrust both throttles forward for a quick burst to overcome any inertia, or wheels stuck-in-a-rut problem.

Still no movement.

Braun was no longer puzzled; he was incensed. He punched his seat-belt loose, opened the top canopy, stuck his head out the top and yelled at the nearest ground mechanic.

"What's the matter with this bloody thing? Are we stuck in a couple of bloody ruts or something?" The mechanic looked at Flying Officer Braun in wide-eyed innocence.

"Sir, you didn't yet call 'chocks away', so they're still in front of the wheels."

The captain's neck reddened visibly.

"Well, get the bloody things out of the bloody way," he yelled.

The two mechanics hauled on the ropes attached to the wooden wedges, yanking them away from the wheels. Braun pushed the throttles forward again, and we lurched forward onto the taxiway.

As we moved rapidly away from the tie-down area, I could now see that the far end of Entebbe's single runway bordered on a heavily wooded area just beyond the threshold. Still, as I had learned from Dennis the previous evening, it was a 4,000- ft paved strip, plenty long enough for the types of aircraft likely to use it, including our Blenheim IV. Nevertheless, after lining up at the runway threshold and receiving permission for take-off, our now steamed-up captain used the 'short-field' method. Applying full brakes, he pushed the throttles forward all the way to the stops, and did not take his feet off the brake pedals until both engines were fully spooled up.

As he released the brakes, the aircraft surged forward, beginning its take-off roll, but even by the time we'd covered the first 200 feet, it became obvious that something was hindering our acceleration.

Our progress seemed labored. In a matter of seconds thereafter, it was evident that we were not accelerating fast enough to reach flying speed before we would run out of runway. By now we were almost half-way down its length, approaching the 'point-of no-return.'

I glanced at the captain. Why didn't he abort? He still had time. His expression remained fixed as he stared ahead. With mouth open and with wide eyes locked onto the trees ahead, his demeanor seemed trance-like.

Then it dawned on me. The gills! They were still open!

I banged on the captain's shoulder and pointed.

"The gills!" I yelled.

He didn't seem to hear me. With his lower lip now quivering in evident terror, his trance-like gaze remained fixed on the trees ahead.

Without thinking about the propriety of my action, I grabbed the gills control wheel that, in the Blenheim IV, nestles in a small console between the pilot and navigator seats. Turning it as fast as I could, I peered out through the starboard window, my eyes glued to those disastrous hindrances to our progress as they slowly flattened out and merged their contours with the smooth curved surface of the engine casings. More agonizing seconds passed as our aircraft then gathered speed and at last lifted off the runway.

Too late. We had little more than thirty feet of altitude by the time we'd reached the threshold. Moments later we were in the trees. We were plowing through the tops, severing branches right and left, the thicker limbs thudding against the leading edges of the wings and slamming into our windshield, cracking it almost at once. Clumps of foliage, diced by our propellers, spread themselves across the windshield, obscuring forward vision.

Engine noise seemed to have increased and taken on an unfamiliar whine. The banging and slapping of leaf-laden branches against the sides of our fuselage rose in intensity as we ploughed deeper and deeper into the enveloping mass of multi-colored foliage.

That was the end, for me at least. I'd already accepted that this time it was curtains for all three of us and, as always, countless episodes of my life flashed through my mind in the split-seconds that we were smashing our way through that unyielding arboreal profusion. I was no longer afraid, however. I had become an outside observer, sitting in judgment of the arrogant sod next to me who'd permitted his foul mood to terminate our lives so pointlessly. I glanced across at his glassy-eyed face once more and resisted a powerful urge to ram my fist into his quivering lips.

Then it was over. Our airplane, evidently not as critically damaged by the encounter with the trees as the noise and the mayhem had seemed to promise, was now flying free. Foliage still clung to the engine cowlings and to the edges of the windshield, but performance now seemed to be more or less normal, and the crack in the windshield had not worsened. At any rate, our captain did not turn back for landing and a review of the damage. He evidently did not relish explaining to the flight control officer how he had plowed into all that greenery. He simply asked me for the course to steer and did not again refer to the matter of the open gills, or the encounter with the trees.

"There's hardly any wind, sir, so 095 degrees should work just fine."

"Thank you," he said. Then, gently, oh so very gently, he eased the nose of the aircraft around in a climbing turn toward the rising sun.

TWELVE

I was angry. Sitting on a chair close to my bed at the RAF Nakuru Station in the mountains above Nairobi, I reflected on the day's events, and on all the other occasions when I'd been in mortal danger, not from enemy gunfire or bombing, but because of incompetence on the part of my own comrades in arms, or in some other situation in which I had no opportunity to contribute to, or participate in, the war effort, nor even in the preservation of my own life. There was never a situation in which I, as a pencil-pusher, could compare my role with that of, say, a fighter pilot, pitting his skills against an enemy flyer, or even a ground encounter where I would face the enemy with a bayonet or even a hand grenade. Rational or not rational, I continued to rail silently against the series of events that had led up to my present frustrating occupation.

Constantly, from the day of my induction into the RAF at Cardington, I'd made it known that I wanted to serve my country as a pilot and, at more or less regular intervals thereafter, higher authority had assured me that my application was being reviewed regularly, and that my turn would eventually be announced. But the more the weeks and months slipped by, the more convinced I became that if I didn't get that course pretty soon, I would not be around when my turn would finally come. I would have lost my longed-for opportunity to make a real contribution. While others were using finely honed skills to pound and punish the enemy in countless ways, I would meet my end while sharpening a pencil or folding a navigation chart.

I began to cool down. "Quit bellyaching," I said to myself. "Your job is to obey orders and take what comes."

I climbed into bed and turned my mind to other things. Soon I was drifting blissfully as Verna was stroking my hair and cradling my head between her yielding breasts.

Despite the frustrated frame of mind of my first days at Nakuru, the opportunity to pass on some of my operational knowledge to help those who would soon be playing their part in one of the most decisive battles of the war, did eventually grow on me. As time went on, I began to accept the fact that even those who merely helped the pilots find their way to the target and back, were doing something that had to be done, and which, however unglamorous and uninspiring, was nevertheless a necessary contribution to the waging of the war.

I began to hone my teaching skills in earnest, and use every opportunity to make my presentations as effective as possible. I asked for and received books on instructional techniques and learned how to make the more abstruse parts of the course more palatable, and the interesting parts, even more intriguing and dynamic. I introduced films that showed navigation and bomb aiming practices being used on operational sorties, and led my students through the actual construction of a course calculator by having them construct working models of their own. And just occasionally, after a particularly demanding session, I would intersperse films, more inspirational than instructional. One of them entitled "Sound-Barrier," in which a test–pilot puts a Spitfire into a vertical dive and keeps it there until he breaks the sound barrier, had always fascinated me and most aircrew members who had seen it.

As the weeks of instruction expanded into months, senior officers of the station began to attend my classes and participate in the exercises I'd been giving my students. Then, at the end of my second month, to my considerable surprise, S/Ldr Wilfred Ames, the station chief instructor, walked in during one of my sessions and quietly parked himself at the end of the last and uppermost tier of the classroom. He did not participate, but when the session was over, he waited until only the two of us remained.

"Why don't we sit and chat for a few minutes," he said.

"Yes, sir," I responded, and sat opposite him at one of the desks.

"That was a very effective presentation, Flight Sergeant," he said "and I'm told that your instructional techniques have been among the most original and effective that this training center has seen."

I mumbled my appreciation of his generous praise, and he continued.

"Have you ever thought of applying for a commission, Flight Sergeant?"

I looked at him, surprised.

"Why no, sir. I was not aware that I could do that."

S/Ldr Ames smiled.

"Would you like to serve as a commissioned officer, Flight Sergeant?"

"Yes sir, I certainly would, but I would like a pilot's training course even more," I replied.

"Oh? Didn't you opt for that when you joined—you are a volunteer, aren't you?"

"It's a long story sir."

"Well, since we're taking this time to review your background, I'd like to hear about it."

I took a deep breath to get my thoughts in order and to call back those long-ago days when it had all begun. I could hear Neville Chamberlain's voice as he broadcast his historic message on that Sunday morning in September of 1939, the whole of Britain listening with rapt attention to his somber tones as he advised us that our country was now at war with Germany.

My friend, Doug Phillips, and I, had gone down to the local RAF recruiting office that same day, and within a week or two we'd boarded the train for the induction center at Cardington. We'd both applied for pilot training, but the recruiting officer had warned us before we left our home-town, that the training centers for pilots were currently fully loaded and, if selected, we'd have to wait our turn. I took another breath and began.

"At the beginning of the war when I enlisted, the training facilities for pilots were swamped with trainees, so when I reported at the Cardington induction center, the Air Commodore in charge of recruiting was already being very selective. When my turn came for the interview, I strode into his office with as much of an air of confidence as I could muster, and marched right up to the front of his desk. He was an impressive officer— large, florid, with a shiny bald head and stern eyes that seemed to look through me. Although he was sitting and I was standing, I had the uncomfortable sensation that he was looking down on me from a considerable height. He came straight to the point:

'So, Layton, you want to be a pilot, eh?' he'd said. 'Have you flown before?'

'No sir. I've done a lot of watching at our local airfield and I know that's what I want to do.'

'Were you in the Volunteer Reserve?'

'No sir. I applied quite recently but I haven't so far had a reply.'

'Well, if you haven't been in the Royal Air Force, what are you doing wearing that tie?'

'This tie sir?' I said, picking up the bottom end of my striped silk neckpiece and studying it as if I'd never seen it before.

'Yes. Don't you know you're wearing an RAF sports tie?'" the Air Commodore said.

I looked up at my chief. "I can tell you sir, he was pretty testy."

I continued. '"That tie is worn only by those who represent the Royal Air Force in a sporting event. How did you get it?'

'I saw it in a shop window. I liked it, so I bought it.'

Then he glared at me and said 'Air-gunner.'

'What was that sir?' I said.

'I said you are classified as an air-gunner. That's all, Layton, you're dismissed.'"

I came out of my reverie and looked up at my chief again.

"Later, I appealed the decision and managed to get myself reclassified, but not for pilot training. I was to be trained as a navigator/ bomb-aimer. My quest for pilot training would have to wait, and I've been waiting ever since."

S\Ldr Ames rose and gathered up the papers he'd brought with him.

"Well," he said "I don't know how much I can do for you about your pilot training application, but perhaps if we can speed up your re-mustering as a commissioned officer, you might have a better chance to make progress with the pilot business yourself."

I looked at him, not knowing what to say.

"And one more thing," he said as he made his way to the door.

"The record shows that you've only been off this station twice since you've been here, and even then it was only two or three hours each time." He studied my face in the way that a psychologist might study his patient.

"I think you could use a break, Flight Sergeant, and I'm going to send you up to Molo—where you can dip sheep with the Trench Family for a few days. Then, as he went through to the outside hall, he turned, giving me that penetrating look once more.

"Drop into my office between classes this afternoon and I'll fill you in on what I've managed to arrange," he said.

THIRTEEN

Molo

In the Highlands of Kenya

I awoke to the clanging of a large brass bell that hung on a scaffold outside the front door of the cabin where I now lay in luxury. From our briefing of the night before, I knew that this rude awakening meant that breakfast would be in forty-five minutes. I rubbed my eyes and began to take in my surroundings.

Looking around, I found that my bed was one of four in a large log-cabin style structure that had two doors at the rear, each prominently labeled 'Bathroom' and I remembered that they led to two fully equipped shower rooms, each with toilets and wash-basins. I also noted that the other three beds were empty and already remade, so I knew my two companions, Alvin and Steve, who'd just graduated from the Pre-Op course, were well ahead of me. Time for action.

As I showered, shaved and dressed, I replayed in my mind the previous evening's events. They had started with the introduction to Mr. and Mrs. Trench and their blond and curvaceous nineteen-year-old daughter, Pussy.

143

Boy that was a name I wasn't likely to forget. Pussy in turn, had introduced us to tall, dark, Elizabeth Dwyer, a tanned and athletic-looking neighbor who'd been invited to join us for the evening meal. After a sumptuous roast-beef dinner, accompanied by a hearty Australian mixture of Shiraz and Cabernet Savignon, Pussy had announced that at breakfast in the morning, she would tell us about the plans she'd made for our day, and that we should be prepared for plenty of exercise. I couldn't wait to hear about it.

A glorious morning sun, still not yet clear of the trees, cast ripples of dazzling light across the path I followed down the slope to the main house. A cool gentle breeze smelling faintly of oatmeal and fried eggs, teased my nostrils as I allowed the wonders of this earthly paradise to seep into my senses. It was England, only more so. The trees taller, the grass greener, the colors more vivid, the songs of the wild-life more haunting and the breeze more caressing than anything I had dreamed or imagined in my whole life. Surely no place on Earth could be closer to Heaven.

Well, as a matter of fact, there was some practical support for that conjecture.

At ten thousand feet above the equator, the Trench farm had to be about as close to heaven as you would find an eight-thousand-acre spread. I pondered that, and resolved that some day, when I would have children I would bring them to see this place, just to give them a taste of the kind of reward they could expect in the next world if they acquitted themselves well enough in this one.

The strident clang of the final breakfast bell brought me out of my reverie. I quickened my pace, made my way to the breakfast room and apologized to all six at the table for keeping them waiting. Then we busied ourselves with oatmeal, topped with bananas and soft brown sugar, followed by servings of eggs, sausage, bacon, and the fried tomatoes that were sizzling on a platter in the middle of the table. Not much could be heard for the next twenty minutes except sporadic murmurs of appreciation and the occasional sound of dishes being passed around the table.

"It's riding today," Pussy announced, as refills of tea and coffee signaled the approaching end of breakfast. "We've got enough horses to provide everyone with a wide choice of the sort of mount you'll be happy with— all the way from spirited to apathetic. So let's make our way to the stables."

The expression on my face as Pussy made that pronouncement, must have told her all she needed to know about my reaction to it—Edith Layton's big son was not into horseback riding. As a matter of fact, I'd never been closer to a horse in my life than the time when, as a kid, I'd fed lumps of sugar to the good-natured old nag that hauled the soft-drinks cart around the streets of Coventry, bringing gallon jars of Stone Ginger and Sarsaparilla drinks to all who could afford them.

Pussy knew all that. Her manner told me that she'd contended with many previous visitors for whom the

Trench farm had provided their first close encounter with horses.

"Don't worry Howard. If you haven't ridden before, I've got just the horse for you," she said, and with that, she ushered us along a broad path that snaked behind the house and up a hundred yards past the guest-lodge to a series of stables. After passing through the gateway that gave access to the stable yard, Pussy led the three of us to a small timber lodge to the right of the stables. A tall, lean Massai at the entrance greeted each of us in turn.

"Jumbo, Miz Trench," he said to Pussy. Then he turned and nodded his head in greeting to each of us. "Jumbo bwana," he said to each, and motioned us to follow him to the stables. It was immediately clear that neither of my companions were strangers to the equestrian world, and Pussy did not take long to sort out suitable mounts for each. While Massai stable-boys strapped saddles on the selected horses, Pussy led me along to a stall near the end of the building.

As we drew near, I found myself looking at a tall, black, fine-looking animal, whose demeanor seemed almost regal. How I was ever supposed to get myself astride such a lofty animal, I could not imagine.

Pussy stroked his muzzle lovingly.

"Let me introduce you to Sam," she said. "He's the best mannered horse in the stable."

I approached Sam with some trepidation and began to stroke his muzzle, too.

"He's so tall, Pussy. How will I ever haul myself up there?" I said, mentally seeing myself making the attempt.

"Don't worry, we have sets of wooden steps for that," she replied. "Here, come take a look." She led me farther along to a small tack room at the end of the building, where all manner of equestrian related paraphernalia were stored. She rummaged around and pulled out a small wooden three-rung step assembly.

"When you stand on this," Pussy said, pulling it out and handing it to me, "You'll find it's easy to throw a leg over Sam's back and sit in the saddle."

"Anyhow, we're just going on familiarization rides today, and I'm going to walk around with you until you're comfortable in the saddle."

I picked up the wooden contraption and mimicked what the others were doing. I took Sam's reins and followed them outside to give the stable boys more space to saddle up all three of them. When they'd done that, I placed the booster in position, and when I felt that no-one else was looking except the stable boy, I mounted the small structure and heaved myself into the saddle on Sam's back, only to slide right off again, from the other side of the haughty creature onto the hard dirt floor. After an interval of a few seconds to assess the extent of the damage to my person, I decided that I was bruised but not otherwise seriously hurt. I struggled to my feet, brushed myself off, and moved back to Sam's left side.

To my dismay, Alvin's grinning face greeted me. He had brought a short builder's ladder and leaned it against Sam's side.

"This way, you won't have to leap at all, mate," he said.

I grinned back at the good-natured Aussie. Then to my considerable surprise, I found myself rejecting the idea of any kind of artificial help to get myself aboard that noble animal.

"Thanks, but no thanks, Alvin," I said. "If I can't get on his back without these contraptions and he throws me when there's no one else around, or if I fall off when I'm out on a ride by myself, how will I ever get back on board again?"

After several more false starts and a few more bruises, I found myself sitting squarely in the saddle on Sam's back, wondering how I would ever get off again if he didn't throw me first.

That first day that will stay with me always, was the beginning of a love affair with the world of horses, but I didn't know that at the time. We spent the whole morning being led around a large outer paddock with either Pussy or one of the stable-boys walking at our sides, giving instruction and answering questions the whole of the time. In the afternoon we did it again, only this time our instructors were also mounted and riding beside us as we walked, trotted, and cantered around an even larger, rutted path that encircled the homestead, guest-house and outbuildings and several meadows beyond. About mid-afternoon, our tutors told us to continue with our riding practice without them—and that they would be meeting us back at the stables at 5pm. Then they left us to fend for ourselves.

To say that I was saddle-sore when we filed into the stables at the appointed time would certainly not overstate my discomfort. And the assurances that we would recover as soon as we got into the saddle the following day only served to persuade me that my best course would be to complain of a sprained ankle and hobble about all day.

And yet . . . and yet . . . after a most satisfying dinner and a good night's rest, followed by an equally sumptuous breakfast the following morning, the aches and pains and indignities of the previous day seemed to have eased considerably. The idea of claiming a sprained ankle had disappeared completely and I found myself actually looking forward to whatever might lie in store.

Pussy, her long blond tresses tied in a bun at the back of her head, a silk scarf knotted at her neck, and wearing her customary garb of jeans and shirt with rolled-up sleeves, made her announcement at the end of the morning meal.

"It's a cross country ride this morning and Elizabeth will be joining us. I shall lead the party, and Elizabeth will be at the rear." She looked around to make sure we were all on board with the plan.

"We'll all meet at the stables at ten o'clock," she said. "But first I have a little side-show for you."

Pussy led us up the path at the side of the house, and around behind the guest–house. There we saw an old stone tower that looked to be about eighty feet tall. It was hard to tell its original purpose, but some time or another in the past it might well have been used to store drying crops. The iron stairway that wound around the outside all the way to the top showed a certain amount of rust in places where its green paint coating had flaked off, but it did not look unsafe.

Pussy led the way up the stairway and we followed her at intervals. From the railed-in concrete top, I looked out at the breathtaking panorama spread before us; lush meadows, multicolored brush, clumps of trees, riding trails and gently rolling meadows, out to far horizons in every direction. I stood there in silent awe of the infinite beauty of all the colors of the rainbow; not the soft and subtle shades of more temperate climates, but multi-hued reds, oranges, and vivid yellows and greens; an unforgettable scene.

"You can see nearly two miles in every direction from here," Pussy told us.

I turned to her. "And how much of it belongs to the Trench family," I asked.

"Everything you can see," she said.

A different pace prevailed at the stables this morning. We'd assembled at 10 AM as arranged. Stable boys, no longer distracted with assisting us with our mounts, had already saddled-up all five horses by the time we arrived, and were otherwise going about their tasks quietly and efficiently. The one-day concentrated instruction of the day before, seemed to have transformed Steve and me into riders more concerned with enjoying the day's outing than with getting on and staying on our means of transportation. At least, that's the way it was for me.

In minutes we were on our way. When she had satisfied herself that we were all mounted and ready, Pussy guided her horse up to the front.

"Let's go," she said, and started off across the compound at a walking pace. We continued in that manner until all the buildings were behind us and we were out on a dirt road that stretched away to the horizon. Then as she broke into a trot, we all followed suit, staying in line behind her. Sam's easy gait made it easy for me to apply what I had learned the day before, and I gradually synchronized our movements. And so we rode on, trotting for ten minutes at a time, then reverting to a walk for another ten minutes, after which we would trot again for a somewhat longer period.

At the end of the first hour, perspiring but happy, I noted that we were riding through an area of gently rolling meadows.

"Let's go," Pussy called again, and with a "Whoopee," she turned her horse off the road and began to canter across the field on our left. Sam followed her without effort. I did not attempt to guide him, for he clearly knew exactly what to do. Nor did I feel any trepidation when Pussy broke into a full gallop and Sam and the rest of us followed.

It lasted for a few exhilarating minutes before Pussy reined in her mount near a clump of bushes and called a halt.

"Break-time," she said. "And for anyone who feels the need, those bushes should serve your purposes."

Elizabeth came forward with a bag in her hand.

"Oranges, anyone?" she offered.

In ten more minutes, we were in our saddles again and on our way back for lunch, but this time, Pussy had us galloping from the start. Again the rush of the sharp thin air in my face and the feeling of unity with my eager steed obliterated all other awareness of the world around me. I reveled in our headlong rush through this limitless paradise, part of me wishing the ride would go on forever, and I knew that my gratitude to Pussy Trench for opening this new world for me would be with me always.

Sam saw the snake before I did. Thick coils, disturbed by the riders ahead, raised themselves out of the long grass. A diamond-shaped head readied itself to strike. Sam skidded to a stop and reared on his hind legs, throwing me unceremoniously into the greenery behind. I was on my feet before there was time to think about it; grabbing Sam's reins and pulling him aside, not, I confess, to help the startled animal steer clear of those deadly fangs, but so that he would not rush off without me.

Elizabeth rode up from the rear. "Howard, are you hurt?"

Hurt? I hadn't even thought about that. I twisted and turned and moved my head around. "I seem to be OK, thank you Elizabeth." Then, thankful that I had spent so much time learning how to get myself onto Sam's back, I put my foot in the stirrup, swung myself up into the saddle and with Elizabeth at my side, cantered off to catch up with Alvin, Steve, and Pussy.

Soon, we were sitting around the lunch table, avidly re-living our adventure.

By this time, we all understood that the close of meal-times was Pussy's opportunity to make us aware of up-coming plans and events, and today was no exception. Toward the end of lunch, Pussy tapped her tea-spoon on her cup, grinning as she rose to make her announcement.

"I hope I didn't wear everyone out today," she said, letting her eyes rest on Alvin, Steve, and me in turn.

We all broke into a spontaneous round of applause.

"Pussy," I said "you're wonderful, and we love you. For my part, I don't know how to thank you for what you've given me in the brief time I've been here with you, and I know my companions feel the same way." I heard them voicing their agreement and saw the color rise in Pussy's cheeks. She looked at me mischievously.

"You just love me for my horses, that's all," she said.

"Pussy, I'd love you if you had only half as many horses," I quipped.

She laughed and blushed again, and I could tell that she enjoyed every minute of all the time she spent providing servicemen with these brief but unforgettable respites from their pre-occupation with the business of war.

"This afternoon, you will be free of chaperones," she told us. "If you wish, you are welcome to saddle up again and go riding by yourselves, the only conditions being that you will use the same horses and will not ride alone. Otherwise you are free to just loaf or do whatever you might most enjoy."

"The bus will be coming for you tomorrow afternoon, but if any of you would care to get up early and help me do a little sheep-dipping, you'll be very welcome."

"Sheep dipping? What's that?"

"I've done a bit of that back home," Alvin said. "It's to de-louse their coats and preserve the quality of the wool. You just pick them up and drag 'em through a trough of disinfectant stuff."

"Well, the chief instructor told me I should have a crack at that," I said, "So you can count me in, Pussy."

"And me," Alvin added.

At seven o'clock the following morning, dressed in a khaki shirt with sleeves rolled up, and wearing my oldest pair of slacks, I stood there in line at the dipping troughs with Pussy Trench on my right. Doing as I had been instructed, I grabbed a bleating animal from the farm-hand on my left. Holding it by its tethered feet, I swung it back and forth through the bath of gray, evil-looking fluid in front of me. Following that muscle-straining exercise, I passed the still bleating and struggling victim over to Pussy. She in turn, went through the same dunking motions, after which she passed the hapless animal to the receiver on her right, who, with astonishing speed and dexterity, removed the lashings from the still bleating creature's feet, and sent it off at a run to the adjacent compound. Pussy then turned to me for the handover of the next unwilling participant in this undignified process.

I stood there in the same spot for an hour and thirty minutes, swinging load after load of live sheep from left to right until I felt my arms and shoulders pulling out of their sockets. By the time Pussy called a halt to the dipping and mentioned something about breakfast, I wasn't sure that I would have the strength to walk up the path to that ever-inviting dining room. But the sight of Pussy, turning away from the trough and striding easily to the pathway, settled the matter. Somehow, I had to stay on my feet and tackle the journey.

Alvin, taller and stronger than I, had been working just as hard in the line on the opposite side of the trough, but he, too, seemed to be having difficulty moving himself onto the north-bound path. To our eternal shame, both of us had to stop after a few yards and rest on a path-side bench, which we later learned, had been placed at that spot precisely for that purpose. Some five minutes later, Pussy, now accompanied by Elizabeth, took each of us by the arm and helped us hobble our way to the house—and breakfast.

That magical few days at the Trench farm sustained me for the rest of my instructional stint at Nakuru, and I tackled my classes with renewed vigor. Whenever I felt I was over-worked, my thoughts would turn to Pussy Trench in her khaki shirt and riding breeches, swinging those sheep through the dip troughs with ease, one after the other; wiping her brow with her sleeve from time to time, blowing wisps of hair out of her eyes and giving orders in her slightly imperious voice; and I would marvel at her energy and determination. Always, those thoughts succeeded in lifting me out of my complaining frame of mind, and I would immerse myself in the business of further refining my methods, and making sure that those eager souls who gathered in my classroom every day would get the best I had to offer.

A few weeks after my return from Molo, S\Ldr. Ames called me to his office.

"How are you feeling, Flight Sergeant?" he asked as I saluted.

"Just fine thank you, Sir."

"Well I think you're due for a change of pace," he said.

"How's that Sir?"

"H.Q. doesn't like to keep instructors here too long. They fear that after a spell of several months here, there's a tendency to lose touch with the operational world."

"Yes I can see how that could be sir."

"Anyway, since you've been hard at work here for more than five months, I've felt it my duty to include your name in the next postings north. We'll miss you here of course, and it won't be easy to fill your shoes in the classroom."

"Thank you very much sir. Your approval means a lot to me." I paused. "May I ask where I shall be going?"

"I'm really not supposed to tell you that, Flight Sergeant, but unofficially, I see no harm in letting you know that Command is looking for a few extra crews to speed up the rate of aircraft delivery from West Africa to the El-Alamein area." He paused to let me absorb that information. Then he continued.

"You'll be leading flights of them across the continent, and I think you'll do a good job of that." He stood, smiled, and offered his hand.

"Thanks for the fine job you've done here, Flight Sergeant. Your posting instructions will be on the notice-board tomorrow."

FOURTEEN

Cairo January 1942

Wing-Commander Carlton-Thomas of the RAF Ferry Command strode in from the stairway and sat on the rail at the side of the deck of the houseboat, looking around at our faces as he did so. Keen light blue eyes set deeply in a tanned, intelligent face, locked onto each man in turn.

"No, don't get up—this won't take long. I just want you to know that some of your colleagues have been complaining about this delivery job." He knitted his sand-colored eyebrows. "Can you believe it? They say that they'd hoped for something more directly involved with bombing the enemy or shooting him out of the skies." He spread his hands to convey his total puzzlement with such unreasonableness.

He scanned our faces again. "Well I'm here to tell you that all the aircraft we have available are doing that right now. They're busy pounding the enemy, and we can't increase that effort until we have more airplanes. Does that make sense?"

There were one or two chuckles as we nodded our agreement.

"Gentlemen, I want you to leave this briefing session with a very clear understanding of the importance of what you are about to be doing."

His eyes moved steadily from face to face again as if to give each of us—some two dozen airmen in all—a personal message.

"This is a crucial phase in the desert war. Rommel's supply lines are stretched to the limit as he attempts to force his way into the Delta area. Because of this, we have an optimum opportunity to destroy his army before he can bring up enough reinforcements to retaliate effectively. The key is to get enough of our own aircraft to the front, to help our land forces do the job swiftly and in the most decisive manner." He paused again.

"We have no time to lose. We need fighters as well as bombers, and since, because of limited fuel capacity, it's difficult for fighters to get here under their own steam, we have to go get them from places where ships can deliver them. In this case, gentlemen, that place is the West Coast of Africa."

There were nods and murmurs of understanding. Some of us had learned about the general set-up from the few RAF crews who'd flown the route before us.

"We're involved in a race against time, and you gentlemen are vital participants in that race. You'll fly without cease for the next few weeks or months. You will fly across Africa, to where fighter aircraft, both British and American, are unloaded from ships, assembled, and test-flown ready for you to lead them in convoy back to this Command. To avoid excessive risk and loss of much-needed aircraft and men, you will fly as far as possible in daylight hours and will make a sufficient number of refueling stops to make that possible. The round trip is more than 7,000 miles, and adds up to between 40 and 50 flying hours by the time you get back." He paused again, glancing around, letting the information sink in.

"When you're in Cairo," he continued, "you'll be quartered on this houseboat, and although you'll be free to move around the city of Cairo while you're waiting for your next flight, I caution each one of you to check the notice board each afternoon at fifteen hundred hours for the next day's roster. If you have any questions at this time, fire away."

A fresh-faced newcomer to the route raised his hand. "Sir, is this a new service, or have others already flown this route before us?"

The Wing Commander smiled. "Don't worry, you won't be pioneers. British Imperial Airways started a basic Trans-Africa route in the thirties, and the Americans added twenty transport aircraft to the route last spring. Since then, we've begun our own little show. The RAF has carved out some of the landing places and staging posts, and the chaps in an outfit called Pan-Am Africa are already improving bases at a number of locations along the route. So if you want to enjoy the comforts of home in the middle of the African bundu, just make sure you arrive at Maiduguri at sundown." He smiled again. Then, as he stood, preparing to take his leave, his expression became serious.

"Just remember gentlemen that your task is an operational one. It is a crucial part of the war. You won't be as exposed to enemy action as elsewhere in this theater, though there is more of that than you might expect. However, there are other hazards to beware of. Much of the trans-African route is dense featureless jungle, alternating with equally featureless desert. Your navigation must be accurate, and you must use every opportunity to top-up your tanks. Too many of our aircraft have been lost because of failure to pay sufficient attention to those criteria. I can tell you, it's not easy to find a downed airplane, even in the open desert, and it's much worse than that in the middle of a dense and endless forest.

The experienced operational flyers among you may wonder why we go to such lengths to give you a good understanding of the hazards you will be facing. 'What's so special about delivering airplanes? Surely it's one of the safest jobs around, isn't it?"

The Wing-Commander shook his head. "Not so," he said, looking around at our faces once more, to make sure he was holding our attention.

"Consider the navigation methods you'll have at your disposal on this route, and compare them with those you are accustomed to."

"Map-reading wouldn't get you anywhere because the terrain is largely featureless. At most landing strips, there are virtually no conventional roads or rivers, towns, railroads or lakes to help you stay on track, so you are left with 'dead- reckoning' and radio beacons.

The latter offer the optimum way to get where you are going, but those you will work with are neither as modern nor as reliable as those you are accustomed to. We're working on that problem, but right now, you must allow for the possibility that one of them may go off the air just when you most need it." He paused again to let us absorb that sobering information.

"Dead-reckoning, your remaining option, can work well if you make sure you have enough fuel to do a little hunting when your destination isn't where you thought it would be. You plot your course very carefully and make due allowance for wind-drift, which is mostly fairly predictable, and you make a careful calculation of your projected time of arrival. The problem is that when you've arrived, there often isn't much there to make you aware of it; a few huts and a wind-sock, and a landing area that is hard to distinguish from the surrounding desert. That's why the Trans-Africa run is no ordinary delivery run, and it is why we've lost too many highly valuable men and machines—even before we began to use it for delivering fighter aircraft.

He stood and paced the deck, frowning. You need to know that this route, which actually extends all the way to India, was conceived and developed for transporting cargo—heavy machinery and essential supplies, using large aircraft whose fuel capacities and operating range were never as limited as those of small fighter aircraft. The use of the route for delivering fighters was not even considered until our need for large numbers of them became a crucial factor in our defense of the Nile Delta."

He stopped pacing and swept the area with his piercing gaze once more.

"I hope I've made my point, gentlemen," he said.

"I'll see you all again in the briefing room tomorrow at 0900 hours. At that time, a couple of aircrews who've already flown the route several times will give you all the information you will need."

He looked around once more at our intense and attentive faces.

"Good luck and good flying," he said. Then he was gone.

That night in my room, I had maps and charts spread all around me—over the floor and across my bed. Carlton Thomas had warned us that we should ready ourselves for departure at any time, but he'd said nothing about the order in which crews would be detailed for the trip. And so far, none of us knew who we were going to be crewed with. What if there was a surprise and we got our orders to fly out tomorrow? What if I found myself allocated to a crew that was due for departure immediately?

Better get some flight planning started.

Where to begin? From what I'd been told, the vast stretches of countryside between our various refueling and overnight stops were pretty featureless. After flying south as far as El Obeid, our course would turn more or less due west, along a line that wove in and out of the southern extremities of the Sahara Desert. Some of the

time, the scenery would comprise little more than sand
dunes and scrub, and at others it would skirt the edge of
the rain belt and we would be flying over half-starved
forests. According to the available charts, the greenery
further west would become thicker and denser until we
got fairly close to Takoradi on the west coast.

One thing was clear. There would be few usable
landmarks between stops, and even the stops themselves
would be nothing to write home about. For the most part
they would be fairly insignificant clearings in the
countryside, populated by single-story native dwellings
and bordered by the airstrips and staging posts where we
would spend the night. The maps showed roads linking
the places we would land, but from what we'd been told,
they were mostly unpaved dirt tracks, and since they
wandered all over the place, we wouldn't be following
them anyway.

Clearly, our dead-reckoning navigation would have to
be good, so I'd better start working on the flight-plan
right now.

The briefing the following morning reassured me.
Flying Officer Ned Twombly, the pilot in charge of the
session, advised us that the trip west would be flown by a
pair of aircraft with an experienced crew in one of them
and a novice crew in the other. The two aircraft would be
in radio contact at all times. On the return trip, each of
the two Blenheims would lead a flight of six fighter
aircraft, but the flights would not necessarily be at the
same time, or even on the same day. Nevertheless, the
trip west would provide us with a valuable opportunity
to familiar ourselves with the terrain and the en-route

staging posts as well as the airfields themselves. I had to agree with our instructor as he paused for a moment to invite questions. The arrangement certainly made sense.

"This is your route in a nutshell, chaps," he continued, and he began to list our refueling stops and mileage on the blackboard:

Cairo – 550 miles-Wadi Halfa

Wadi-Halfa-450 miles-Khartoum

Khartoum-225 miles-El Obeid

El Obeid-325 miles-El Fasher

El Fasher-195 miles-El Geneina

El Geneina-508 miles-Ft Lamy

Ft Lamy-135 miles-Maiduguri

Maiduguri-350 miles-El Kano

El Kano-525 miles-Lagos

Lagos-375 miles-Takoradi

TOTAL   3638 statute miles (Map 4)

"All right, question-time everybody."

Twombly looked around the room and motioned to a navigator just behind me.

"Yes, Pilot Officer?"

"Sir, I see from your list that one of the legs is only a hundred and thirty five miles. Why would it be worth refueling after such a short distance?"

Twombly smiled. "Good question," he said.

"It introduces my favorite topic. Bear in mind that the planes you are leading back east are Hawker Hurricane fighters. Since they will be the Mk 1 version, they will have a maximum range of 600 miles, which is less than your Blenheims; so take another look at the staging-post chart. Let's say they topped up at Kano and then made straight to Fort Lamy instead of refueling at Maiduguri—no, that's not a good example. You'd be off your heads to bypass Maiduguri."

There were chuckles around the room. "Aside from Maiduguri and Accra, the Hurries don't have the range to bypass any of the other listed staging posts. In any case, many of these stretches don't give you much room for error as it is." He paused.

"Given the variable wind conditions you will encounter, and the limited opportunities to get reliable fixes, there's a higher risk of going off course for a while––so it's important that you use every opportunity to top-up."

He smiled. "Just remember our motto in this outfit: 'Fuel in the tank is like money in the bank." He paused again.

"There's another consideration to be taken into account," he said. "The problem of transporting fuel to the various airfields en route is difficult and costly, so that at some locations, they will ration you and you won't be able to get a complete fill up. So the golden rule to follow is to get as much as you can, whenever and wherever you can, OK?"

Satisfied that the point was well understood by all concerned, our briefer picked up his notebook and walked out of the room. "See you later chaps," he said as he went out the door.

Most of us turned up again at sixteen hundred hours to get the 'Gen' on our scheduling. The roster, posted on the notice-board as promised, told me what I needed to know. I was to join a crew that would be taking off in three days. The pilot, P/O Gregory Holmes, was the stocky chap who'd been asking questions at the morning's briefing. I made a note to myself to spend some time with him so that we wouldn't be strangers when we got together in the airplane. The pilot of the other aircraft with the experienced crew on board was Flying Officer Geoffrey Smart, and I noted that both crews were detailed to report to the briefing officer at nine hundred hours on the day before the flight. That would be 48 hours from now. I'd better get moving.

The mail-rack caught my eye as I turned away from the notice-board. There was a letter from my mother and another official looking envelope. I tore it open.

"This is to inform you that you have been granted an acting commission in the Royal Air Force, with the rank of Pilot Officer . . ."

Whoopee! Old Ames had really meant what he'd said. Perhaps now I would have a better chance of getting my pilot's training course. I rushed out and bought myself a couple of battle-dress blouses with the shoulder tabs on them to accommodate the officer's stripes, and a couple of shirts with similar provisions. The formal officer's uniform would have to wait 'til after my return from this first trans-Africa trip.

I strutted around the deck of the house-boat, hoping someone would comment on my new status, but no one yet knew me well enough to have noticed the change. I went to the bar in the officer's mess to celebrate my promotion as a party of one, and I sat there alone at the counter, drinking Crown Royal and thinking of Verna. Boy, wouldn't she be proud of me now! Of how hard I'd worked, and what I'd achieved. She would be sitting there at home, just longing for my return; longing to have my arms around her. She would forget all our differences and how I had lied to her and ducked out of our wedding at the last minute. Yes, she would forgive me now. Surely.

My thoughts drifted as I savored the possibilities.

"You're a new face around here. Haven't I seen you somewhere before?" I looked up, startled. It was the voice of Wing-Commander Carlton-Thomas, the officer who'd given us our first briefing. I stood up, flustered.

"Well sir, I just got notification of my commission, and this is the first time I've been in this officer's mess—in any officer's mess."

"Well, I'd like to be the first to congratulate you, officer. What's your name?"

"Layton, sir—Howard Layton."

"Well, let me buy you a drink, Pilot Officer Layton. What'll it be?"

"Er, yes, thank you sir. Canadian Club and ginger-ale would be fine."

The Wing Commander ordered my drink and another for himself.

"I'm afraid I disturbed you Layton," he said. "You seemed very pensive. Are there some questions troubling you regarding your work with this outfit? If so, perhaps I can help."

Although by then I was no longer clear headed, I was not so far gone that I failed to see and seize the opportunity that his words offered.

"Well sir, to tell you the truth, it's something else … "

I told him the story of my quest for a pilot's course, detailing the promises that had been made to me, and the years I'd been waiting for some indication that my turn had come. In my cups, I dwelt on my conviction that I could serve my country far more effectively as a pilot than as a navigator. He listened politely, but the only promising comment I remembered as he finished his drink and took his departure was that he would put a word in for me.

"Meanwhile," he concluded, "Good luck with your aircraft delivery missions."

I went to bed, and back to my reverie, persuading myself that Verna would forgive me; that when I confessed and begged her for her forgiveness, things would work out. Yes, somehow they had to.

FIFTEEN

January 1942

We were flying fairly high to make the best use of the prevailing winds. At thirteen thousand feet, it was out of the north-east at 40 miles an hour, which gave us a quartering tail wind of about 28 miles per hour and a ground speed of around 200 mph. Our flight leader, Flying Officer Smart, seemed happy with that compromise between get-there-itis and reasonable fuel economy. Wadi-Halfa and Khartoum were behind us, and we would soon be landing at El Fasher. A half hour later when we began our descent, I began to wonder how anyone could be expected to find anything in this desolate environment. This was still desert, and there was very little vegetation to be seen in any direction. Eventually down to 2,500 feet, I asked the leader's navigator whether he could see any sign of the air-strip.

"Not yet," he said. "And we'll have a hard time spotting it even when we get there. The landing strips are just hard-packed sand, so keep a good look out. Right now we're just trusting the NDB radio beacon."

At about 1,200 feet, our lead aircraft banked to the left, changing course by some 30 degrees. Then I spotted it—nothing more than a long stretch of discoloration in the light brown panorama, and a small bunch of buildings at one end. We entered a circling pattern to make an approach into what little wind there was. Then, to my surprise, I heard F\O Smart instruct our pilot to land first, while he made one more circuit.

In a few short minutes, we were on the ground, and I was getting my maps and charts together. Then I heard Greg's voice again.

"Howard, you go on ahead while I fill in my log-book. I'll only be a few minutes. Oh, and while I think of it, don't bother with your kit, they'll send transport for that later."

Transport for my kit? That seemed odd. I wasn't accustomed to such service. And why was Greg sending me on ahead?

I climbed out of the cabin, slid off the wing and began to walk across the apron of hard packed sand toward the wooden operations hut about fifty yards away. A group of airmen, sitting on a bench at the front of the office, waved in welcome.

A sudden great weight on both of my shoulders stopped me in my tracks. I stood there frozen for a moment, unable to make sense of what had happened. Then as my brain began to get into gear again, I turned my head slowly to the left and found myself staring at a large yellow paw planted firmly on my shoulder. A moment later I felt a thump on my back. My knees buckled.

As I lay on my back in the dust and opened my eyes, I was staring at the shaggy head of a real live lion whose paws were planted firmly on my chest. The creature began to lick my face. In my dazed condition, I was conscious only of the extreme roughness of the animal's tongue and the conviction that its intention was to tear off my facial skin as a prelude to making a meal of me. A powerful animal odor assailed my nostrils as I lay there, trying unsuccessfully to make sense of what was happening.

The ordeal was over almost as soon as it had begun. The lion, tired of licking me, trotted off. As I turned my head toward the flight hut, I could see where it was headed. I could also see the same friendly group of airmen almost bursting their sides with laughter at my plight. I struggled to my feet and made my way toward them. In moments the Flying Officer in charge was greeting me with a hearty handshake and advising me that I had just been inducted into their mascot's fan club and was now a member in good standing. He grinned at my evident puzzlement about the situation.

"You might as well get used to the idea of meeting strange mascots at these staging posts," he said, "Just wait 'til you get to Geneina."

Later, as we assembled for the ride to the Mess for lunch, it dawned on me that my rendezvous with Leo had been carefully planned. I now understood why our leader had ordered us to land first, and why Holmes, the pilot of our own Blenheim had delayed his exit from the aircraft to fill in his log book. I learned that despite the fact that Leo was known to reserve his special greeting for strangers only, these pranksters, knowing what I was in for, had not wanted to risk spoiling it.

In just about two hours we were off again to El Geneina where we would have dinner and spend the night. This proved a better staging post, and with a paved runway set in an area of fairly dense undergrowth, it had not been as difficult to find as El Fasher had been. Nevertheless, we soon discovered that supplies were harder to come by at this location. Shortly after we'd landed and fortified ourselves with a mug of hot, sweet tea, we were each handed a .303 service rifle and requested to set forth into the bundu to bring back meat for the common larder.

The idea was that although there was already plenty for us to eat for dinner tonight, our job was to replace that bounty with meat for those who would arrive during the following days. That seemed an equitable system, and three of us set off in a truck with a guide named Singman and his four assistants, who wore flowing white galabias and white head-dresses.

As we drove south the woods thickened, and soon we'd left the last evidence of human habitation behind. In less than half an hour our driver pulled over onto a smooth dirt patch at the side of the road and parked. Retrieving our rifles and ammunition from the back of the vehicle, we followed our guides into the dark greenery.

I didn't know what sort of animals we were expected to encounter in these mid-African woods, but to my surprise, we spotted a very deer-like creature soon after we'd left the dirt road. I turned to Geoff Smart, a more experienced sportsman than I.

"What was that, Geoff?"

He put his fingers to his lips to indicate that we needed to make less noise.

"I think it was an antelope," he said quietly.

The head guide shook his head. "No, no officer. Is a deer, a red deer."

"Didn't look very red to me," I said.

"You will see when we kill one. It has some red," he insisted, and the other bearers nodded their heads in agreement.

As we progressed, we encountered more of these deer-like animals and before an hour had passed, Geoff had brought one down, Sure enough, its hide showed dark reddish-brown areas on the lower parts of its body.

Our bearers tied the animal's legs in the conventional manner so that it could be suspended from a stout tree branch and supported on their shoulders. I was not as good a shot as Geoff, and we continued our stalking in the rich dark greenery for another half hour or so before I got lucky and brought down an animal so large that I wondered whether we would ever be able to carry it back to our truck while there was still enough light to do so. This one, too, had the same dark reddish-brown area on its underbelly.

Since the light was now rapidly fading, we called it a day and made our way back to the truck. By the time we'd humped the animals onto the back of the truck, the sun had set and we made our way back to the airfield in a blackness relieved only by our vehicle's less than adequate headlights. Staying on the dirt track that served for a road took all of our driver's concentration, but Geoff made it seem like a joy ride by joking about our afternoon as if it had been a grand safari.

"It's no wonder you managed to get that deer, Turner. It's so bloody huge that there was no easy way you could have missed it." I grinned, content with the day.

"Geoff, old bean, you're just jealous, that's all."

Our contribution to the station larder was applauded by everyone as a generous return for the hospitality we were receiving. At dinner we washed down our food— which in this case, was some sort of tasty African hare— with Egyptian 'Stella' beer. All in all, we had a pretty good evening.

The following morning I was awakened by a muffled banging on my cabin door. "Coming," I said.

I climbed out of bed and shuffled over to the door, eased it open a bit—and decided I must be dreaming. The head of a large giraffe almost filled the doorway, and on seeing me standing there open mouthed, pushed its muzzle forward to fully open the door. Then, extending a long thick tongue, it proceeded to lick my face.

It was not until I related my experience to my host at the breakfast table that I learned that the friendly beast happened to be the station mascot that I'd been warned about.

Well, I supposed, if El Fasher could keep a nearly full-grown lion around the place as a mascot, one could not complain about El Geneina's giraffe. But my morning encounter proved to be just the beginning. Before breakfast was over, the station chief, Flying Officer James Parker, tapped me on the shoulder.

"How did you enjoy your visitor this morning?" he asked.

"Well, he certainly woke me up," I replied. "But he should change his brand of tooth-paste."

"Oh that was just the beginning," he said with a perfectly straight face. "The rites-of-passage at this station include a ride on Lofty's back."

An hour later, I found myself lining up on the so-called 'parade ground' for my turn at climbing aboard the giant creature, and in watching the attempts of others to climb on its back, it became obvious to me that getting aboard, difficult though it may be, was not to be compared with the task of staying there. To manage that long enough to indulge in anything resembling a 'ride' seemed infinitely more difficult—and even dangerous. Happily, a reprieve came at the last minute. Our imminent take-off schedule took precedence over the ritual, so we were granted a postponement of our initiation until the return trip.

That, of course, was the problem. A total escape from the various rituals in force at these staging posts was highly unlikely because everyone knew that we would have to pass the same way again on our return trip.

By 0900 hours, we were on our way. Since the remaining 1, 800 miles to Takoradi was a bit too far for a prudent one-day schedule, we would spend the night at El Kano, which meant, alas, that our stop at Maiduguri would be for refueling only. We would not revel in the luxuries of that well-known staging post until the return trip. So it was that our two Blenheims landed at Kano in time for a late lunch—and also to learn that we would be delayed there for at least another day because our leader's aircraft had developed hydraulic problems.

No hardship. Accommodations at Kano were well organized and comfortable, and the food was pretty good. Moreover, there was a town to visit, with a bazaar and well equipped sports facilities. Over dinner, Geoff raised the subject of the morrow's activities.

"If they stand us down for tomorrow, what about the four of us going into town? We could do a bit of shopping and see what else this great metropolis has to offer." He looked around at our attentive faces

"For that matter we could go watch a polo game, or even get to play it."

"Polo?" I couldn't believe it.

"Oh yes, Kano is well known as the polo center here."

I was intrigued. "This I have to see," I said. "Let's do it."

After making the rounds of the Kano bazaar and purchasing snake skins that we might never have a use for, we made our way to the sports arena and sat watching a polo game in progress. The ponies seemed to have some sort of sixth sense about what was required of them and appeared as much involved in the excitement as their riders. With the game over, and the winners declared, an official approached us.

"I hope you enjoyed the game," he said.

We nodded our heads. "This is the first time I've seen a polo game," I told him. "It must be very difficult to maneuver the ponies into the best positions to hit the ball the way you want it to go."

The official smiled. "Why don't you all get a bit of first-hand experience," He said. "This is a public field and the cost to participate is quite modest."

I stared at the grinning official and then at the others.

"I wouldn't have the vaguest idea what to do."

In turn, Greg Holmes and Tony, one of the Hurricane pilots, shook their heads.

"Not my cup of tea."

Smarty broke in. "Come on chaps. You may never get another chance like this. It'll be something to write home about." I looked at him, astonished. Could he really mean that? People spent years at that sort of game, just learning to stay on a mount that was making sudden stops and turns all the time, even before they'd have a chance of hitting the puck in an otherwise empty field. But my evident disbelief in what he was suggesting seemed to fuel Smarty's conviction that we should have a go.

"Tell you what," he said. "I've never played polo before, but I'll bet each of you five pounds to one that I'll stay on my pony longer than any of you city boys. Whadyasay?"

"What if nobody falls off?" Tony asked.

"Then I'll owe you all five pounds apiece," Smarty replied.

"Well," Greg stood up and hitched up his slacks. "Nobody's going to get away with a challenge like that. Let's get started."

Sitting astride my first polo pony was like nothing I could have imagined. Never in my past life had I sensed such total indifference to my presence. I knew immediately that my pony had no intention of playing anything but his own game, and that my presence or absence on his back mattered not at all. The game got off to an energetic start within a few short minutes, and served to confirm the conclusion I'd reached.

A bell rang somewhere and my pony charged off with a suddenness that came close to ending my involvement in this happy little conflagration right there. He followed what they called the 'puck,' which was actually a wooden ball, though how he had managed to figure out where it was, I couldn't fathom. I concluded that he could smell it. Anyhow, upon reaching the vicinity of the puck, he somehow managed to maneuver himself into precisely the right position to enable me to wield my mallet and hit it in the direction required. His skill and positional accuracy were such that unless I were a total idiot, I could not fail to send the puck in the direction required to foil the opposition, or even score a goal. That meant that the outcome depended, not on any polo-playing skill or aptitude that I could have demonstrated, nor even on any beginner's luck that might come my way. No, the outcome would depend entirely on how well my pony did his stuff.

Polo, it seemed to me, was a match between the animals involved, and had little to do with the skill of the riders. Which was why, at the end of the game, I didn't know whether to feel satisfaction or vague disappointment about the successes and failures in which I had participated for the previous couple of hours.

At the close, I'd lost some modest amount of money, but nothing to complain about, and my companions had fared similarly. All of us agreed, however, that despite the confusion, our time had by no means been wasted. We'd had a good time and some good exercise. Besides, we could now boast that we'd actually played the game of polo— and that we were therefore polo players. Not everybody could make that claim.

The following day we completed the west-bound phase of our mission, landing at Takoradi in time for a late dinner and a briefing for our return trip.

The Gold Coast of Africa, as most of the western bulge of that continent was known, proved a far more attractive place to visit than I'd expected. Ocean breezes and modest rainfalls, coupled with sub-Saharan vegetation and rocky terrain, all served to provide a comfortable and temperate environment. These factors, together with the well-organized RAF and American (Pan-Am Africa) services, effectively neutralized any misgivings we might have expressed when the Station

Traffic Chief advised us that the six Hawker Hurricanes my aircraft would lead had not yet been test-flown, and that we could expect our departure to be delayed for at least another day. We swam and sunned ourselves, and wandered around the docks and the local markets, and in the evening used the opportunity to put in some extra briefing time with the designated Hurricane pilots.

After dinner in the briefing room, Smarty took charge again.

"OK, chaps," he said. "Let's get to know each other. I'd like each one of you to state your name and give a one sentence description of how you got to be here. I'm going to call out each one of your names in turn." He looked around the briefing room at the attentive faces. "Tony Simpson," he said. "You first."

"I'm Tony Simpson," the tall, gangling young man said as he rose to his feet. "I don't know what I'm doing here. I just got through my pilot's course and completed bombing and gunnery when they told me I was posted overseas." He looked around. "So I don't have any operational experience at all." Every one applauded.

"Welcome to Primary Operations," A voice from somewhere put in.

"Ok, Anton Walbrook, you're next," Smarty said.

Anton, also tall, thin, and sporting a Ronald Coleman moustache, stood up, grinning. "No relation to the actor," he said. "I was with the Polish Air Force. I asked to be posted to the Middle-East because I have friends here in the RAF, and I hope I shall be able to catch up with some of them."

"Who, for instance?"

"Well there's Stefan Landau. He's the best pilot I know. He's with one of the desert squadrons."

"We'll look him up when we get there."

"Aubrey Mason, what about you?"

A somewhat older pilot of medium height and muscular build with blond hair slicked back neatly, rose in response to the query. "I've done one operational tour over France and Germany, and they've sent me here for a bit of a break," He said. "Doesn't seem to me that it's going to be any easier than what I've been doing." He looked around the table. "But I have no complaints." There was a chuckle all round.

"And I don't mind the change," He said, and sat down.

"Stan Carter, you're next," Smarty said.

And so it went as each pilot introduced himself.

Smarty thanked everyone for their short speeches, and wished us all good flying.

"Chaps," he said as a closing comment, "I cannot over-emphasize the fact that our most important task throughout the long haul back to Cairo will be to ensure that we take every opportunity to top-up our tanks. We have no requirement to turn up in Cairo on any special day or at any special time. Our task is simply to make sure that we all get there."

We all nodded that we understood, and Smarty continued.

"You will lead the first half dozen Hurricanes, Holmes, and I expect to follow you with another five Hurries a few hours later. Have a safe trip."

Then he added, "If I don't catch up with you all along the way, I'll see you in Cairo."

At 0600 hours on the morning of January 14, we were in the air and headed east to Lagos, Kano, and on to Maiduguri. We did a careful check at Kano to determine how much fuel had been used to make the trip, and how the predicted fuel consumption of the Hurricanes was panning out in relation to the calculated usage rate. The results were as expected, close to the calculated fuel burn, and therefore satisfactory. But the safety margin left something to be desired. There was no room for significant error. We would have to be careful.

We landed at Maiduguri with some daylight to spare, and reveled in the four course dinner that the Pan-Am Africa facilities provided. Soup, salad, a venison main course, and fruit-cup dessert was followed by snifters of Hennessy brandy for those who cared for it, and an extensive variety of alternatives for those who didn't. Breakfast the following morning consisted of orange juice, oatmeal, bacon and eggs and unlimited quantities of rich, flavorful coffee. We left well satisfied with our stop-over, and ready for whatever adventures might befall. In forty-five minutes we were circling the airfield at Fort Lamy, lining up for our turn to land, and thereafter taxiing over to the service apron for the top-up. Greg Holmes walked down the line of aircraft, talking to each Hurricane pilot in turn.

"Be sure you make a thorough check for water in your tanks. Rock the wings back and forth to be sure it all sinks to the sump. Take your time."

On Thursday morning we were off again, this time to tackle the 500-mile stretch to El Geneina. We would have to pray that the prevailing wind, now forecast at about 5 Miles per hour from the north-east at ten thousand feet, would not become stronger.

An hour and a half into the flight, a little past the 'Point of No Return,' we compared notes over the intercom. All aircraft reported normal fuel burn, and the ADF showed Geneina directly ahead. We droned on.

I glanced across at Greg. He seemed serene and relaxed. I checked in with each hurricane pilot in turn.

"How's your fuel looking Tony?"

"I'd say about right, leader— a bit below half."

"Anton?"

"About the same."

The other Hurries in their turn reported satisfactory fuel levels.

I signed off with everybody, "Over and out."

We seemed to be in good shape, and on course. So why was I uneasy? What was nagging at me? I glanced across at Greg again, and as I did so, he caught my eye.

"What's up, Turner? You seem ill at ease."

I grinned and loosened my collar. "It's just this feeling I have that I'm overlooking something." He continued to study my face for a few seconds, then went back to flying the airplane. I looked at the ADF (Automatic Direction Finder) display again. Nothing wrong there; no deviation of the needle; just straight up and down as it was supposed to be.

Or was it? I continued to stare at the needle, willing it to tell me what was wrong with what I was looking at.

Then I saw it. The needle! It wasn't supposed to be straight up and down. It should have been pointing at one o'clock to allow for wind drift. Then I realized that I was actually looking at its tail rather than its head. The head was actually pointing straight down—as if we'd already passed the Geneina Non-Directional Beacon (NDB)!

How could that be? I grabbed the Azimuth knob and turned it. The needle swung lazily from side to side as if there were no signal. No signal! That was it. We were not receiving a signal! Either our ADF receiver was malfunctioning or Geneina's NDB had gone off the air. I could feel the blood draining from my face as the significance of that discovery dawned on me.

I twirled the control knob back and forth several more times, not willing to believe that there was really nothing there; not willing to face the fact that our primary means of finding the Geneina air-field had disappeared.

I leaned across to Greg, tapping the ADF instrument dial with my right hand.

"We seem to have a problem," I said. "We've lost the Geneina beacon."

Greg played with the control knob just as I had done. He rocked the azimuth back and forth and finally shrugged his shoulders and went back to his controls.

Then, glancing across at me he said coolly, "You'll think of something, Turner." and fell silent.

Well, if there had been any thought in my mind about sharing the problem and the responsibility, Greg's words had made it clear that I had better think otherwise. I was on my own. I was the flight's navigator and the sudden loss of radio guidance was a circumstance that I was expected to cope with without distracting the pilot from his own primary responsibility of flying the airplane.

The knot in the pit of my stomach tightened. Horrifying thoughts flashed through my mind. We would fly on and on while I would be trying desperately to identify landmarks which would lead to the Geneina airfield. I would grasp at landmark straws and give course corrections to the pilot, one after another until our charges would run out of fuel and glide silently to their doom in the unforgiving wilderness. And I would be entirely responsible for the deaths of a group of young, trained, and eager pilots, and for the loss of all of the priceless contributions that they might otherwise have made to our war effort. I, too, would share their fate, but unlike them, I would die in the desert in disgrace.

No! It must not happen. I breathed deeply to shake off my terror. I began to get my brain into gear, examining the alternatives available to us. I would pay attention to essential dead-reckoning and map-reading, of course, but I would force myself to think rationally. First, no one would be allowed to run out of fuel and land without control. If worse came to worst, upon the first report from a Hurricane pilot that he was near empty, we would select the best camel tracks or other landing site we could find, and all of us would then make forced but controlled landings, hoping that the sand would be hard enough so that at least some of us would not nose in. We would not be marooned. We had lots of communication gear between us, and by the law of averages some of them at least, would survive the less-than-optimum landing conditions we would encounter.

With that option reasoned out, I began to feel better—– more in control of my reasoning powers. I turned my attention once more to the ADF display. Still no signal from Geneina. Time to look for others. I remembered the document on navigation aids we'd been given before we set course, and dragged it out. But the list was shorter than I'd thought. El Obeid – EBD; Geneina – EGN; El Fasher – ELF; Juba – JUB. That was it. It didn't look promising. El Fasher was the nearest beacon, and that was 200 miles away. There had to be something closer.

Greg noticed my pre-occupation with my navigation kit. "Found any answers yet, Turner?"

"I'm getting there," I told him. "But I'd like to tell you what I think we should do if our luck runs out—that is, if we don't find El Geneina in time." I could tell he was listening with interest and concern as I went over my plan with him.

"I didn't think you were serious, Turner. When the ADF went out, I just assumed you'd tune in to another beacon somewhere around the place, and we'd be back in business. Are you telling me there aren't any?"

"The nearest is El Fasher, and that's two hundred miles beyond Geneina," I told him.

"And according to the good book, even the well-powered stations are only good for fifty to a hundred miles."

Greg pondered that for a moment. "So what else do you have in mind?" he asked.

"If you're OK with my last-ditch forced landing scheme, I'll try to find a way so we won't have to use it."

He nodded his agreement, and I checked in again with the Hurry pilots. All were now around the quarter mark. I'd better come up with something soon. The minutes slipped by as I worked my way through the frequency band, praying for a needle deflection as I did so. Nothing.

I tapped Greg on the shoulder. "About El Fasher," I said. "Didn't you mention once that one of the other navigators had once tracked El Fasher out-bound nearly all the way to Geneina?"

"Well yes, but getting a signal when you're practically there is not much use, is it?"

As I thought about his words, I knew what we must do. We must make directly for El Fasher and hope that we would get a signal from the Fasher beacon while there was still time to use it to backtrack to Geneina. I told Greg what I had in mind and he agreed that it offered the best chance of finding Geneina that we could hope for.

I tuned the ADF to the ELF frequency and let it stay there. We would take our chances. We would get a signal in time or, if not, we would carry out the forced landing as planned.

I heard Greg's voice again. "We're getting close to our ETA. Perhaps we should start a 'pattern search' for the field."

"The problem with that is that it's very fuel-consuming and we won't even know that we've come far enough," I replied.

"What do you suggest?"

My heart was beating too fast and I was having a hard time concentrating.

I tried to latch onto a mental picture of our situation.

"So long as we keep going on our present course, which I believe to be fairly much on the nose, we'll be better off, even if we overshoot and have to turn back to get to Geneina."

"How would we be better off?"

"Because we would be getting closer and closer to Fasher and have a better and better chance of picking up the beacon. If we got it even for a short time, it would be enough to orient ourselves to backtrack for Geneina."

Then I added, "And that still doesn't interfere with the forced landing plan if we don't make it to the field. If we do pick up the Fasher beacon, we'll be able to give rescuers a better idea of where we are."

The minutes ticked by. I turned to Greg again.

"I think we should go up to twelve thousand."

He looked surprised. "That will take more fuel."

"But it will increase our chances of getting the Fasher beacon sooner."

He considered that for a moment. "All right, I'll buy that."

We notified the Hurry pilots and began a steady climb, leveling out on course at twelve thousand feet. We continued on course for another ten minutes, but the ADF remained lifeless.

Cold sweat dripped off my brow as I turned to Greg again. "Let's go to fifteen."

"They don't have oxygen installed yet. Don't you remember?"

"For the amount of time involved, I don't think it's going to matter."

Geoff gave the order to the Hurries and we began another climb.

I heard Tony's concerned voice over the intercom.

"I'm pretty close to empty. What's the score?"

I was about to reply when, as we crossed the fourteen thousand feet mark, the ADF came alive. Following an initial swing left and right, the arrow stabilized at ten o'clock on the dial. A stronger wind than forecast had pushed us about five miles off course.

"We just got a signal, Tony" I told him, my voice as matter-of-fact as I could manage.

"Just hang on old chum, while we back-track to Geniena."

Following Greg's 180 degree climbing turn, and after making due allowance for wind-drift, I gave him the back-track course for Geneina. The climb ensured that the ADF would hold on to the Fasher signal as we tracked away from the beacon. For twelve agonizing minutes there was nothing. Then, in the distance, the faint outline of the Geneina strip became visible. I listened to general cheering from the Hurry pilots as I announced the sighting, and I became aware of the gradual easing of the tension in my gut.

Shamelessly, despite my agnostic beliefs, I offered silent words of gratitude to whoever was up there. Then Greg's voice came through. "Not bad, Turner," he said, and I could see his head nodding up and down in quiet approval. Oh what sweet words. My chest heaved. I had never had a more gratifying moment in my life.

The intercom came alive again.

"My engine just quit," Tony's voice was edgy.

Silence for a moment, then Greg's voice.

"Hang in there, Tony old chap. Just trim for your best glide ratio and we'll stay with you. Do your best to stay on course." He paused. "Hurries two and three throttle back and stay with Tony." Another pause.

"Hurries four, five and six stay up here with us. Keep an eye on the others below and report any drift off course to Leader. Leader will concentrate on keeping the airfield in sight."

One by one the acknowledgements came back.

"Roger from Hurry two."

"Leader from Hurry three, roger."

"Roger from Hurry four."

"Hurry five, roger."

"That's roger from Hurry six."

We watched Tony's aircraft and his two escorts start down on the long glide to wherever Tony's un-powered flight would take him. As the minutes passed, we, too, were descending steadily without losing sight of the Geneina strip. Greg reported to the Geneina controller that we were inbound for landing and declared an emergency for Tony. He also requested that the fire tender be ready for Tony's probable touch down short of the field.

Tony's voice came on. "I have the field in sight but I'm not going to make it."

"Roger, state intentions Tony," Greg replied.

"I have eighteen hundred feet to go. I'm going off course in a minute to pick the best landing spot I can find."

"Roger Tony, we'll be with you," Greg replied. "All other Hurries line up for landing. We can't risk you running out of fuel, too. Leader will take over escort for Tony."

We watched the rest of the Hurries peel away and take up their positions for the landing approach. Greg throttled back, staying behind Tony by weaving first to the left and then to the right. I watched as Tony finally straightened his flight path for a landing approach along a stretch of almost white sand that ran parallel to a row of gorse bushes. I saw his landing flaps appear at the trailing edges of his aircraft's wings. He must have had his mike locked on because I heard him muttering to himself.

"By God there's wheel tracks along here. Sand looks pretty hard. Let's try wheels down and see how it goes."

193

I saw the sand flying in his wake as he eventually touched down, and I held my breath as his landing run progressed. More clouds of sand billowed, thickening as he ploughed along whatever ruts there were. Then finally, a ground-loop as he came to rest in the densest cloud of all. As my line of sight slowly cleared, I could see that he had not nosed over. Tony was safe and, incredibly, his aircraft appeared safe, too.

"Hurry one has landed," he reported over the intercom, and a medley of cheers drowned out anything else he might have added.

Our landing at Heliopolis evoked more cheers from other crews we met in the debriefing room. News of our adventure had traveled fast, and when we'd done with our debriefing and gathered in the officer's mess, Tony's quick decision to put his wheels down after his last minute sighting of camel tracks, earned him a goodly share of cheers and beers. Wing Commander Carlton Thomas, who'd come to the mess especially to greet us, strolled over to the table where I was sitting.

"Well, Layton, I'm glad to see that you're all safely here. I hear that you had an interesting time of it, and that you did well." He cleared his throat. "I shall certainly have to do my best to help you with that pilot's course you're after."

"Thank you, sir. I must admit this trip was more of an education than I would have wished."

He laughed. "Well, we'd better make the best use of your services while you're here, because I'm afraid we're going to lose you sooner than we expected."

"How's that, sir?"

"They're looking for reinforcements for El-Alamein close-support duty for the final show-down, so since we're now able to deliver aircraft faster than they can use them, we've got to give up some of our crews." He took another swallow from his tankard.

"Since you've only done one trip so far, I expect we'll be able to hang on to you for at least one, or even two more delivery runs," he said, "but keep your eye on the notice board after the next one."

The notice-board at the house-boat had welcome news. We had three days off before we were to stand by for the next delivery run.

There was also a letter from my mother. I tore it open.

"Howard, my darling, it breaks my heart to tell you this, but it will only hurt you more to go on hoping. I spent the evening with Verna a few nights ago, and I asked her why she hasn't been writing to you. She told me frankly that she is bitter and heartbroken. She said that when she'd talked with you on the phone during the last weeks before the wedding date, your responses were somehow tentative and your original enthusiasm for the marriage seemed to have cooled. She was left wondering whether you really wanted to marry her. Then when she bumped into Ida one day while she was shopping in Broadgate, and learned from Ida that Doug had a full week off before he was posted overseas; that everyone in the RAF got at least a few days off before any overseas posting, her suspicions were confirmed. Verna just isn't the type to come running after anyone, regardless of how much she's hurting, Howard. I tried to persuade her to write to you, but she refused. She said that since the time of the car accident, she's always felt that you would be marrying her out of pity because of the scar that remained under her right eye, and that when the wedding date drew near, you decided you just couldn't go through with the pretense. I know the scar's only a little thing Howard, but Verna's a beautiful girl and in her mind it's a major disfigurement. She said that if you had married her, she would never know whether it was out of pity or not. She's very proud and she didn't want any part of that, nor will she permit anyone to try to change her mind. She's a stoic, you know, and she was adamant that she never wants to see you again." I fumbled for something to blow my nose, and read on.

"Howard, you didn't even tell me you could have had that leave to come home for the wedding before you went abroad. I don't know what to say to you. I am very hurt, too. I don't know how you could treat that poor girl so cruelly. That's not the way I raised you, Howard. I pray you will write to me and tell me that it is all a terrible misunderstanding . . ."

The words blurred. I folded the letter and stuffed it into my breast pocket. For several minutes I stood there in a daze, unable to digest what I'd just read. Then I made my way to my room, pulled the letter out of my pocket, and read it again . . . and again.

If it had been possible for me to climb aboard an airplane right then, to get to Verna's side as quickly as possible to beg her for her forgiveness and attempt to bridge this gulf between us, I would have done so. But it was not possible. Apart from having lied to her and caused her so much emotional pain and misery, I'd been a quarrelsome and over-sensitive suitor as well. It was natural enough that in the course of time, Verna had come to realize that a future with me was simply not worth waiting for. In the end I'd got exactly what I had long deserved, and there was nothing I could do about it. It was over.

I sat there, slowly facing up to the real root of the problem between us, and I came to realize that although our actual age difference had been little more than six months, and although in most cases, that would not have mattered, Verna, by the time we'd met was already a mature young woman with a balanced and realistic view of life. She had been older for her years than most. I, on the other hand, had been hardly more than a willful and irresponsible child—and a very spoiled one at that. True, we were both older now, and our levels of maturity might well be to some extent converging, but I was realistic enough to realize that the damage already done was irreparable and that there was just no way it could be undone. I tried to picture the future we would have had together if Verna had not already had the sense and the maturity to face up the truth herself. For once, I looked at it squarely and objectively, not sparing myself the sad truth it presented. We had been born at the wrong times for each other. It was as simple as that.

I went to the bar and ordered a double Canadian Club without the ginger ale. I followed it with another and another, and prayed that the Wing Commander would not again catch me in my cups.

SIXTEEN

El Alamein

The final battle of November 2nd, 3rd and 4th, 1942, at El Alamein, marked the culmination of a four-month long struggle during which each side had occupied itself with the task of building up supplies that would enable it to prevail in the ultimate bid for possession of the whole of the British Middle East Protectorate. The conflict as a whole had been a drawn-out struggle encompassing many major contributing battles fought by Australians, Canadians, South Africans, Indians and other members of the Commonwealth, as well as English, Irish, Welsh and Scots, whose combined efforts would now settle matters once and for all. Everything that the might of the Axis powers could bring to bear on this battle of El Alamein was now pitted against all that the Anglo-American alliance could itself marshal against the enemy.

These days and nights in late October and early November of 1942, would see the end of the struggle of the last several months, and would mark a decisive turning point in the world conflict as a whole, more so than anyone in the European theatre would yet realize.

The raids that we in 223 and 55 squadrons were now undertaking were part of that struggle. We were supporting the Eighth Army's newly achieved domination of the battlefield, and the all-out effort that would culminate in Rommel's final flight from the North-African scene.

The location of the battle was ordained by the fact that the area measured about forty miles from north to south, and stretched from the coastline to the northern limit of the Qattara Depression, a vast, below-sea-level tract of dark brown quick sands, impassable to men and machines alike, that stretched for a further hundred miles to the south. This made the Alamein tract to the north of the depression a logical last ditch choice for the defense of the Nile Delta and the British Middle-East presence. The fact that the area was close to the British supply bases and that it also stretched Rommel's own supply lines to the limit, served to support the logic of that choice.

In the air, supplies of British Blenheims, Wellingtons, and Hurricanes were now augmented by American twin-engined Bostons, Baltimores and B25s. These longer range aircraft were making their way to the Western Desert under their own steam, while the shorter-range Hawker Hurricane and Kittyhawk fighters were shipped by sea to strategic locations outside the war-zones and flown into the Western Desert area by routes such as I had so recently been flying.

The Kamsin seems to be blowing sand all the time here, despite the fact that it's out of season. And it's not only in my eyes, it's even under the sheets in my bunk. The tents we have here are mostly the army bell-type, and for some reason they don't seem to keep the sand out very well. It gets under my sheets and my pillow so that the scorpions don't know when they're out of bounds. In fact, when I awoke this morning, I found that I'd been sleeping on a big fat scorpion. It lay there all squashed on my pillow, and I must have turned my head onto it when we were both asleep. At any rate, I was thankful that my thick head of hair had saved me from its potent stinger.

Actually, I don't really know where I am, but judging from the time it took the truck to get us here from Cairo, I would estimate that 223 squadron, where I'd eventually been posted from the Trans-Africa Run, was now parked with 55 squadron and several other front-line support squadrons about twenty five to thirty miles west of the Nile Delta. This would place the location about ninety miles east of the El Alamein front, concentrated between the Quattara Depression and the Mediterranean coast.

If we flew direct from here to Rommel's front lines we could be there in about half an hour, but we didn't do that. Instead, our route took us northwest over to the coast, then we turned due west and followed the coast until we were in a position to line up for a short southerly bombing run over the coastline to the enemy's concentrations of artillery and armor, and to the fuel trucks and dumps that constituted our targets for these final days of the El-Alamein struggle (Map 5).

Our second flight this morning, like the first one on this late October day, had followed that pattern and had been highly successful. Our airplane, piloted by P/O Harland, had flown in the left wing of our flight of six Baltimore aircraft, staying in fairly close formation as we followed our leader, Wing Commander Horgan. We approached the target, identified as LG21, from the sea, flying a southerly weaving course to confuse the enemy's anti-aircraft batteries. Dense, black smoke puffs peppered the sky around us, and as I glanced to my left, I could see that a series of holes had ripped across the starboard wing of number three in our flight. Moments later, a violent lurch of our own aircraft indicated that a shell had burst just below us. Then our leader straightened his flight path for the final bombing run— the most vulnerable minutes of any bombing mission.

We're sitting ducks now, prime targets for the ground gunners, and as their aim steadily improves, the black puffs around us get closer and appear in dense clusters. It now seems that we're all getting hit and our pilots are finding it increasingly difficult to maintain a steady course. Thick smoke is now streaming from the fuselage of one of the aircraft on our starboard side. In a moment, it falls out of formation.

The barrage stops just as suddenly as it started. The ground gunners have found another target. Two Hawker Hurricanes shoot across the target area thousands of feet below us, machine-gunning the anti-aircraft batteries and the fuel trucks as they go. Black smoke everywhere. The target is now ours.

All eyes now on the leader, opening our bomb-doors as we see him open his; watching for the moment when his bombs fall clear. I almost hear the lead bomb-aimer lining up for the strike.

Left! Left . . . left . . . right a bit . . . steady . . . steady . . .steady . . . steeeadeeee!

Bombs gone!

As I see the leader's bomb-load leave the belly of his aircraft, and wobble their way down in clusters, I press the release button to jettison our own contribution to the barrage.

Then a sharp diving turn to the left with throttles wide open, and we're putting distance between ourselves and the target as fast as we can.

In another hour we've landed and are being debriefed—and thirty minutes after that we're eating a late lunch, to stoke up again for our third strike of the day.

I'm so tired, I'm almost numb. We're all tired. We go about our business in a sort of daze, all our actions automatic and assured through the numbing daily routine that gets the job done. Tomorrow we'll repeat the performance, the targets much the same and the outcome just as predictable. It is the end. We know it, every Brit, Indian, South African, Australian, New Zealander and American knows it, and the enemy knows it just as surely. It is palpable. It is in the air.

The afternoon arrives. Our Baltimore has been re-fueled and more bombs and ammunition have been stowed aboard. We take off again, trundling down the endless stretch of flat hard sand that is our runway, heave our heavy bomb-load into the air and climb to the rendezvous area to get into formation once again. The route is the same as the early morning flight of the day and the mid-day one as well, and the bombing run results in the same black clouds of destruction on the ground and in the air around us. For the third time that day we revel in that exhilarating dive away to port as we leave the scene at speed, and offer up our thanks for another day of survival. We pray that our pilot will stay awake long enough to get us down in one piece, and despite our fatigue, we shall be in the mess-tent by six o'clock for a few cans of ale before sloping off to our cots, too far gone, even to eat a sandwich.

When the rays of the morning sun ripple across the dunes again, we'll be at it once more. One, two, or at the most, three more days. By then, that legendary soldier, Field Marshall Erwin Rommel, will know that his defeat is already a fact of yesterday.

It is November 13th·and the enemy has been in flight for several days. Hurricanes and Kittyhawks have taken over the task of providing air support for Montgomery's Eighth Army as it now takes up the westward chase once more. Both 223 and 55 squadrons have been stood down, taken off operations for a much-needed respite for men and machines. Our status has been switched to training-mode in preparation for an eventual move west. And, for a precious while, there will be rest. Oh how welcome that word. Even the contemplation of it is a balm in itself.

For a couple of days, most of us just ate and slept and visited the medical officer for check-ups. In the evening we passed the time quietly over Pilsener or scotch and soda, contemplating the newest rumor that we would have time on our hands for perhaps two or three weeks.

As our fatigue gradually left us and strength and zest for life returned, we began to take an interest in opportunities to occupy our time. We learned that daily passes were now available for trips into Cairo and Alexandria and that a regular transport schedule had been established to get officers and men to and from the big cities, to the flesh-pots, casinos, and cabarets. We hoped El Badia would be able to accommodate us all, and that El Groppi would be able to make enough Sfogliatella to satisfy all the ice-cream lovers who would now descend on their famous establishment.

Soon, I began to attend to the letter writing that I hadn't had time or strength for over these recent weeks. I told my mother as much about events as I thought the censor would tolerate, then I wrote a few lines for my brother, Archie, somewhere in Europe, entertaining the troops with his magical music.

Then there was Verna. What would I write to her? Would I be able to persuade her to write to me again, to give me another chance? It had been so long since I'd seen her cherished hand-writing on an envelope that I could not now imagine what I could write that would interest her, what pleas I could pour from my heart.

'Verna my darling, I know from your long silence that it's useless for me to hope any longer for your forgiveness— for all the disappointments and sadness I've inflicted on

you, but couldn't you just write to me as a one-time friend who longs for just a few lines to let him know how you are doing? It would mean the world to me, and I have to believe that it would mean something to you, too, to show a little forgiveness. I love you Verna, my darling, and I shall not give up hope.'

I read it through once, twice, three times. Then I tore it up and flopped onto my cot, fully clothed. In a few minutes, I slept.

Mindful of the fact that from this time forward there might be many more periods when I would have time on my hands, I knew I would need some diversion to take my mind off Verna. I would learn a foreign language, I decided. French or Italian or both, and it couldn't hurt to throw in a little Arabic, too. Sitting with Flying Officer Stefan Landau at breakfast the following morning, it occurred to me that he was just the chap to give me advice on my newest quest.

Stefan, I knew from overhearing him in the mess, was fluent in French, and since his friend, Anton, had managed to meet up with him and had told him about our adventures on the trans-Africa trip, Stefan and I seemed to have got along pretty well.

"Stefan," I said as I passed him the coffee dispenser, "I'd like to do something for myself while we have time on our hands, and I've been thinking of studying one or two languages. I've heard you speaking French in the mess tent, so I would welcome a bit of advice from you on how I might go about learning it."

He smiled his favorite sardonic smile, and rose from the table. I could sense his chest puffing up a bit.

"Well now," he said, looking down at me from his lofty height, "I would have never believed that I, Stefan Landau, Viceroy of God, would be asked to take on a role as menial as that of a school-teacher."

I was about to reply but he held up his hand, calling for silence. "But for a friend, I will in this instance accept that role. I will tell you exactly what to do, and each time I give you the benefit of my wisdom and infinite knowledge, you will buy me two beers. Not Stella bloody Pilsener, mind you," he added "but Bass at the very least."

I nodded my agreement and laughed. "Are you going to give me tests and make me do homework if my performance is not up to snuff?"

"Oh no," he said. "It's much easier than that. You will purchase a French-language copy of Victor Hugo's Les Miserables or some such, and with the aid of a French-English dictionary, you will read it from cover to cover." He wagged his finger at me. "And I, Stefan Landau, will take you aside on random occasions and quiz you on what you have read and understood."

A day or two thereafter, I took the morning van into Cairo and set about my shopping. I had no trouble finding 'Les Miserables' at one of the bookstores along the Sharia Madabegh, and shortly thereafter, I found a used copy of Ketteridge's English-French dictionary at a bazaar. For good measure, I added a couple of trashy modern French-language romance novels, and from that day forward, I buried myself in my project whenever the opportunity arose, sometimes not emerging from my tent for a whole afternoon or evening.

At intervals of about a chapter or so, I consulted with Stefan to check on my progress. True to his word, he took the time to listen to my halting efforts to recount the story paragraph by paragraph. He painstakingly corrected my efforts to pronounce the words, if not correctly, at least with something approaching an intelligible accent. And, of course, on each occasion, the session was followed in the evening by payment in the form of bottles of Bass beer, as promised.

Later, to enhance my rate of progress, I bought a couple of books on the grammar of the language. With this at my side I began to get a better understanding of the story of 'Les Mis,' as well as French grammar. By this means, as the days passed, I could sense that my pre-occupation with my studies was bringing about a slow but definite healing. My thoughts were not as constantly focused on Verna during the day, and in the evenings there was always alcohol to diffuse the ache in my stomach and heart, and deaden my awareness of loss and guilt.

I wanted this time of study to last forever, but it was not to be. Before the month was over, I learned that I was to be transferred to 1437 flight and given two weeks leave, after which I was to be ready at a moment's notice to take a jeep and a team of bomb disposal experts on a drive west as far as Castel Benito airfield in Tripolitania.

I promptly took a ride into Cairo again, back to the Sharia Madabegh bookstore, and bought myself an

Italian–English Dictionary. Since the store-keeper himself turned out to be of Italian origin and evidently well educated, I sought his guidance on what other books I would need for a 'crash course' in his language. He guided me to a couple of 'Italian-for-the-tourist' type books. Then, after I'd made my purchase and was about to leave the store, he said, "Perhaps I can give you something to remember from your first brush with the Italian tongue. There is one sentence which some consider the most beautiful in our entire language. Would you like to hear it?"

"Yes please, Signore. It will be a sort of souvenir for me to take away as a reminder of my visits to your store."

"I will write this down for you," he said "Here it is." He read from a book he'd pulled off one of the shelves:

"Mia madre ha sessant anni, e piu la guarda, e piu me sembra bella."

The lilting Italian pronunciation, with its drawn-out emphasis on the esses, ems and els, had a roundness and beauty that I knew would be lost in the English translation, which he then gave me. "My mother is seventy years old, and the more I look at her, the more beautiful she seems to me."

I smiled at him appreciatively. "Thank you Signore, I shall always remember this introduction you've given me to your beautiful language."

SEVENTEEN

It's Thursday morning, the day after my visit to Cairo, and I'm at breakfast with the Viceroy of God. He's lecturing me again.

"Turner, sometime very soon, we'll be moving west. Nobody knows when we'll be in this area again, so you'd better see all you really ought to see—the things you will want to tell the folks about when you get back home."

"Well, I've already seen the sights of Cairo—the Pyramids, Shepheards Hotel, and Mena House. And like everybody else, I've entertained the girls at Badia, and watched them drink water from bottles I've paid for as champagne."

"Have you been to Alexandria yet?"

"No, as a matter of fact I haven't, and perhaps I should do something about that."

"Better get on with it, Turner. Time is running out."

I checked the Mess notice-board for the 'shopping-bus' timetable and scribbled in my name for the ten o'clock departure. The day was already sparkling and for the time of year, quite warm, when we pulled into the first stop near the beaches. A visit to the beach and a good romp in the deep blue waters of the Med seemed like a good way to introduce myself to the delights that the city had to offer.

I headed for the officer's swimming club on Sidi Bishr and once inside the pavilion, I changed as quickly as I could, ran across the silken sands, and plunged into an endless train of warm, boisterous breakers that tossed my torso and limbs about as if they were just parts of a rag doll. I swam and swam, reveling in the confluence of sun and salt water, and the boundless well-being that I was suddenly aware of.

I didn't even notice that there were no other swimmers sharing the velvet waters with me. Just adults and children, paddling in the shallows and looking for pretty shells. A huge wave burst over me, scraping my body over the coarse sand below, sucking me a little further out to sea as it crested. I gave myself to the power of the surging waters and to the ease with which they tossed my body from the crest of each towering wave to the roiling sands below. I felt my back and my sides being scraped along the rough sea-bed and I knew that at that moment I was as alive as I ever would be.

The real significance of what was happening—that the raging currents were taking me further out to sea with each crest— did not dawn on me at first. I simply reveled in the bracing waters and the joy of being alive. When I eventually realized what was happening, I turned and began to swim steadily for the shore, but it wasn't long before it became obvious that I just wasn't making any progress. I increased my effort and swam with all the strength I could muster, but I soon realized that my frantic flailing was getting me nowhere.

I made a conscious effort to calm myself and apply some reason to my predicament. I turned and swam steadily again, but this time parallel to the shore instead of directly toward it. I remembered from some past instruction I'd received, that the best chance of getting out of an adverse current was to swim across it rather than against it. As I persevered it did seem that I was holding my own, and after some minutes, I ventured a turn toward the shore again. Convinced that I was now getting a little closer, I turned back to the parallel course for a few more minutes, before trying for the shore once more.

Wrong. I was making no progress whatever. I was not, as I had believed, working my way out of the current and toward the sands of that golden Alexandria beach. Despite swimming with everything I had in me, I was being swept further out to sea with every stroke.

I saw a solitary figure on shore, a shapely girl with long black tresses, waving her arms at me vigorously, but her image steadily receded. Her hair, blowing freely in the wind, was the last I saw of her before another mountainous wave tossed me yet further out to sea.

Doggedly, I continued my attempts to swim out of the current until exhaustion forced me to stop. I grasped my swimming trunks at the waist-band and worked my way out of them. I, hoisted them over my head and waved them as high above the water as I was able, until I could wave no more. The shore-line disappeared from view, and aware at last of the total futility of my efforts,

I gave myself up to the rhythmically beating waves. I trod water, drifting in quiet peace.

What a silly way to die after surviving so many of the perils of war. To be snuffed out, not even in the act of contributing to the war effort. Would anybody really miss me I wondered. Come to that, was I really worth anybody's tears? No, I decided, I'd loused it all up this time around, so perhaps it's just as well that I'm being taken out of circulation, before I do any more damage.

I miss you Verna, and I hope you'll miss me, too— just a little. I'm thinking of you in my arms once more as I say goodbye to this world. I'm burying my face in your honey-colored hair and rubbing my nose in that little bunch of grapes at the side of your pretty head. I cup your beloved face in my hands, and kiss you tenderly. Oh those lips, how they set me on fire. With the tips of my fingers I'm gently caressing the nipples of your soft breasts. The waves throw me back and forth as I move my head down between those lovely mounds, and press them both close to my cheeks. Oh my darling, if only I could tell you how I love you at this moment.

The motion of the waves is more insistent now, as my head moves down again and I kiss your navel tenderly. My passion rises as my hands move over your satin hips, then down toward the center of your womanhood. I lose myself in my reverie. I'm raising my head now, kissing your soft, parted lips again. I'm pulling you toward me, burying myself in the mystery of your sex; moving with the waters as they toss our unresisting torsos to and fro; bonding our bodies tightly together as I wrap my arms around you, then wrenching us apart, crushing and wrenching in ever more urgent cycles as our union harmonizes with the undulations of the restless sea. The rhythm and the pounding of the waves continue toward a great crescendo as my reverie explodes in a cataract of rapturous convulsions. Oh, my darling, darling girl.

I revel in the crash of one last monstrous wave, and I'm bursting with laughter, wild and joyous laughter, as a world of raging water closes over my head.

EIGHTEEN

God, how my head hurts!
I sputtered and gasped for air as I shook off my delirium, aware that something or someone was hitting me on my head. With eyes now opening, I'm astonished by the fact that I'm still alive.

"Ecco! Prend! Ecco!" Another slap on the head. "Ecco!!"

I turned my head slowly and painfully to see a motor launch close to my right shoulder, and a large muscular Adonis-like creature holding the other end of the oar that is still tapping me on my head. Still only half conscious, I reached up and grabbed this link to the world of the living, and found myself being hauled steadily toward the safety of the launch. In minutes I was sprawled on its deck with a towel slung over my nakedness.

Slewing the boat around and gunning the engine, Adonis set course for the beach and in a while we pulled alongside a jetty near the beach cabins. As I staggered on to the boardwalk, clad only in a towel, the girl with all that hair began raging at me again.

"How could you be so stupid? Didn't you see that the black balls are up?"

I glanced across at the poles she was pointing at, and for the first time noticed the huge black balls perched on top of them.

"What do they mean," I asked tentatively, gradually getting myself together.

"You're supposed to know that when you swim here," she replied vehemently. "When they are up, there is no swimming. The currents are too strong and very dangerous. I would have thought that at least you'd wonder why nobody else was swimming."

I looked down at her intense face, and her shapely form, and decided that I was very fortunate that someone as beautiful as this girl should care enough about my welfare to be storming at me in this way.

"Thank you for your concern," I said. "You have a big heart, and I'm glad you went on at me." Then in an attempt to account for my lapse of common sense, I added "I'm in the RAF and this is my first visit to this beach since I've been in your country."

Her expression softened. "Well, now you know," she said. "My name is Gabriella, but you can call me Gabri. What's yours?"

When I told her my name, she looked me up and down and commented. "You're a good looking man, Howard, but you're skinny. You need to do something about that. Anyhow, since you're new here, I should at least offer you a little hospitality. Would you care to join my friend and me for a sandwich?"

"If I'm not intruding, I would like that, thank you Gabri," I said. "But first, I'd like to hop over to my cabin and put some clothes on—to hide some of my skinniness."

She grinned at me impishly. "Oh you still look pretty good to me, even if you do need a little feeding up."

We strolled over to a large pavilion, behind which were several rows of sizable cabins. Gabri led me to one of these.

"This is where we'll have lunch when you're dressed," she said.

Soon thereafter, fully clothed once more, I found myself seated at a trestle table, watching the beautiful Gabri take delicious looking cold-cuts, Italian bread, and a variety of peppers and other greens from a large hamper. A bottle of Chianti followed, together with some fine cutlery and glassware. She laid places for three persons, and a few minutes later I learned who the third place was for. The Adonis-like creature who had rescued me came through the door just as Gabri began pouring the wine. Gabri smiled at me and then at the new-comer.

"Let me introduce Ercole," she said "That's Italian for Hercules. Ercole, this is Howard."

Ercole, who, I decided, was very aptly named, turned his Godlike head in my direction and looked me over. Nodding slowly, he settled his massive body onto the bench at the table and began to help himself to the cold-cuts. Conscious of my lean and hungry appearance in Ercole's presence, I excused myself as soon as we'd had our fill of the exquisitely prepared lunch. Gabri took me aside and pressed a piece of note-paper into my hand.

"Call me when you come to Alexandria, again." she whispered.

"What about your friend? Won't he object to my presence here a second time?" I countered.

Gabri batted her long black eyelashes at me coyly. "No, no" she said, "He's been my bodyguard since I was a baby, but he's not my boy-friend or anything like that."

Then as I turned and trudged across the sand to my own cabin, she called after me.

"See you soon, yes?"

"Yes," I called over my shoulder, and hated myself for what I was saying.

"I could have told you exactly what would happen," Stefan told me at breakfast the following morning. "She sensed you were vulnerable and she was right."

"But how could she know," I argued. "We'd just met."

Stefan smiled at me in his favorite avuncular fashion. "Women are like that; they just know."

"So what am I supposed to do?"

"Far be it from me to advise on matters of the heart, my friend, but if it happened to me, I would treasure it as a means of helping me to bear the loss of the girl I loved so much." He paused, and for the first time since I'd known him, I could sense a genuine concern for my plight.

"Let yourself go, my friend. See where it takes you. Help yourself heal in whatever way the good Lord offers.

That won't make your loved one any less precious to you, but it will help you to live with your loss."

I considered Stefan's words and studied his concerned face.

"You know, Stefan," I said "I'm beginning to see that you are a real friend," I searched for words "and well, I--- just didn't expect it."

Three short days later, I joined another party of aircrew members heading for Alexandria and the beaches, and on arrival at the same pavilion I'd visited previously, I telephoned Gabri, using the number she'd written on the paper she'd given me so surreptitiously.

"Who is this?" she asked in her beguiling musical voice.

"Can you come to the beach, Gabri?" I asked her.

"Oh, it's so good to hear from you, Howard, but I can't come this morning. I have to wait for a call from my mother. She's in Cairo. Why don't you come up here. If you've got a pencil and paper, I'll give you the address."

I scrambled frantically for something to write on, grabbed a newspaper from the seat beside me and scribbled in the margin at the top of the page as Gabri gave me the information. A minute later, I set off in search of a taxi, and ten minutes after that, I found myself on the sidewalk of a quiet suburban street, looking up at the entranceway to a well appointed apartment-building.

Shortly after I'd pressed the button, a buzzer signaled that I could enter. Polished brass and the pungent odors of a variety of cleaning agents greeted me as I made my way across the foyer to an ancient–looking elevator. Gabri opened her apartment door in response to my ring. A white, loose-fitting garment, ending just above her pretty knees, and supported by slender shoulder straps, revealed her shapely neck and throat. It struck me that she was well aware of the raw sex-appeal of her appearance. Her black tresses hung freely down her back, and I quickly found myself fantasizing about what it would be like to bury my head in the loveliness of those burnished glories of feminine allure.

"It's nice to see you," she said, taking my swim-wear bag from me. "Do please sit down while I make some coffee." With that, she led me across a rich Persian carpet to a well-worn, over-stuffed settee.

"Please sit and relax, and I'll be back shortly." She disappeared through a door behind me, and I was left to contemplate my surroundings. Somewhat church-like were my first thoughts as I looked around again. Subdued lighting and stained-glass windows coupled with mahogany paneling, spoke of conservative taste combined with some affluence. I wondered who'd been responsible for creating this quietly attractive and restful retreat.

Gabri appeared shortly with a tray bearing two cups and saucers, a pot of coffee, containers of cream and sugar, and a silver platter of sugar-coated crackers. She sat beside me and remained silent while I reached for one of the delicacies.

"How old are you Gabri," I asked, as she began pouring the coffee.

"I'm eighteen, going on nineteen," she answered. "And I'm old for my years," she added.

"Why do you say that?"

"Because most people I come across every day seem so child-like—and that includes you." She grinned at me mischievously.

I considered that comment, and yes, she did seem more composed than most girls I'd known. Almost all-knowing, in fact.

We chatted awhile, learning a little about each other.

"Is your mother away for long, Gabri?"

"Well, Cairo's where we live, really. This apartment is a sort of retreat that we mostly use in the summer, but I like to come here whenever I'm not in school."

"Where do you go to school?"

"The English Mission College."

"Ah, so that's how you come to speak such beautiful English."

"Oh yes, they're very strict about that. They expect us to speak better English than the English in England."

"Well, that wouldn't be much of a challenge. At home, we speak the worst English of the English-speaking world. When we travel within the British Isles, we often have a hard time understanding each other."

"I didn't realize it was as bad as that."

"Well, take countries like Canada, the USA, or Australia. They're much larger than Britain, but you can understand what people are saying, and make yourself understood anywhere you go in those places. It's not like that in Britain."

She nodded her head and smiled. "Let's not talk any more for now," She said.

We sipped our coffee.

A few more moments of silence, then Gabri put down her empty cup. Turning toward me, she reached up and took my face in her two hands and kissed me gently on my lips, slowly and repeatedly. Then more firmly, parting her lips, she kissed me with more passion. As I was about to respond to the sheer bliss of the affection she was showering upon me, she paused and took a deep breath. Sitting back, she took my hand in hers and for several long moments, she sat motionless, looking into my eyes steadily and intently. I sensed there was something special she wanted to say, and was having difficulty finding the right words. Eventually, she dropped her gaze and rose to her feet holding my hand.

"Hold me Howard," she said quietly, "I want to whisper in your ear." I took her in my arms and stroked her long, lustrous tresses. We stayed like that for a short while—I, holding her close and feeling the warmth of her body and the beating of her heart; Gabri with her upturned face nestled against mine. Then she whispered.

"Howard"

"Yes"

"Howard, I . . . I want you to make love to me."

"I ah, what was that Gabri?"

"Yes, Howard, I really did say that," she whispered, "I want you to make love to me."

"Gabriella, you're beautiful and it's enchanting to be with you, but we're still really strangers. We don't know anything about each other." I looked down at her earnest face, "Besides," I added "I'm deeply in love with someone else."

She spoke again, this time not as tentatively.

"In ordinary times, Howard, I would never have said those words to any man, but these are not ordinary times. You will be gone in a few days—and I know that I want you to be the first to make love to me."

I grappled with that revelation for a moment or two.

"Are you telling me you're a virgin, Gabriella?"

"Yes and I want you to be my first lover."

She looked up at me and held my gaze.

"I knew that when I first saw you Howard. I caught only a brief glimpse of you when you arrived at the beach in your RAF uniform the other day, and were on your way to the changing booths. You had that air of reckless abandon as if you didn't care whether you lived or died, and I knew I wanted you. However fleeting it had to be, I wanted you. Whether you care to believe me or not I've never felt like that before. That's why I was so frantic when I thought you were drowning and I was about to lose what I wanted to experience so much."

"Really? And there I was, convinced that all that shouting and arm-waving on the beach, was just humanitarian concern."

Ignoring my banter, she paced the room slowly, head down, left hand holding her chin. She seemed to be collecting her thoughts as if in preparation for a profound speech. At length she stopped in front of me and tossed her head.

"I want a memory, Howard, a beautiful memory, whether I ever see you again or not." Her gaze became intense. "I don't believe in pretending," she said. "My father used to tell me 'Life is too short. Make up your mind what you want and get it when you can. Mostly, the chance comes but once, and you'd better be ready.' I've come to understand that, Howard, and that's how I plan to live my life."

She stood back then at arms length, her eyes holding mine. Her voice became softer, her manner more tentative again.

"For God knows what reason, I want you to be the one to give me my first experience, Howard. The first time is so important for a woman. It stays with her and can influence her attitude to intimacy for the rest of her life." Then she whispered, "I know it will be beautiful with you."

I just stood there, not knowing what to say. I shook my head slowly.

"Gabri my dear, I . . . I just can't . . . you're so beautiful, but it's . . . well, it's just a very difficult time for me." Then repeating myself, "and we don't know a thing about each other."

She nodded her head a little, acknowledging what I'd just said. She took another step away from me, talking to herself again. Then she turned toward me once more and spoke, almost mockingly.

"So what are you going to do now, Howard? Walk out, just like that?" She slapped her hands against each other in a funny little wiping motion. "Won't you wonder when you go home to England and look back on this day, whether in your masterful restraint, you robbed yourself of a very special memory?" Her eyes flashed as she continued.

"What if you don't make it out of this war? What if your plane comes spiraling down out of control one day? Won't you have a fleeting thought for what you missed today? Won't you wonder whether your virtue was worth the loss of the brief but honest intimacy I offered you today—love that you cast aside as you proudly walked out through that door?"

Her lustrous eyes still holding my gaze, she eased her loose white garment off her shoulders and let it fall to the floor.

"Well?" Again the challenge in her eyes as I gasped at the ineffable beauty of her now totally unclothed body.

"Make up your mind."

I gazed at her lovely form for several more seconds, etching in my mind every nuance and shadow of its wondrous curves. Then I picked up my swimming bag and strode to the door. I turned at the threshold, the words spilling out of me.

"Gabriella, you're wonderful. I'll remember you the rest of my life."

For another long moment I let my eyes feast on her beauty. Then I turned away and closed the door behind me.

Down at street level, I made for the corner near the taxi-stand, and stood there in a sort of trance.

A voice somewhere at the back of my mind nagged at me.

'Are you trying to play God, Howard? Are you presuming to judge what is best for that mature girl, who certainly seems very clear about what she wants?'

'A girl of eighteen or nineteen hasn't got much idea about what is good for her.'

'And you have?'

'Stop going on at me, I'm confused enough as it is.'

'All right, I'll stop, but I warn you, you're going to fret about this for the rest of your life. You're always going to wonder what it would have been like to share just a few hours of bliss with that wonderful creature who offered herself to you so honestly.'

'Anything else?'

'Yes—oh never mind. If you still can't see the light. Do what you will.'

A taxicab turned the corner and eased up to the curb in front of me. The driver called through the open window.

"Where you like to go Effendi?"

I stood there in a stupor, just gaping at him.

"Effendi?"

I found my voice. "Will you be here again in, say, fifteen minutes. I'm ah, waiting for a friend."

The driver nodded.

"Bukkra fi mish mish," he called as he pulled away from the curb.

"Allah be with you." Then he was gone.

Mish mish? Where had I heard that before?

I paced slowly back and forth on the pavement at the corner, head down, hands clasped behind my back, wrestling with confusing thoughts. Stefan's words came back to me. 'Let yourself go, my friend. See where it takes you.' Could I do that? Wouldn't that just create a complication I would later regret? I went on pacing. Fifteen minutes ticked by as Stefan's words continued to nag me. 'Help yourself heal in whatever way the good Lord offers. It will help you to live with your loss . . .'

Thirty minutes passed.

Her door was already open when I stepped off the elevator and made my way back along the corridor to her apartment.

As I entered, Gabri, still as unadorned as when I had left her, looked up at me with smiling eyes.

"I was waiting for you."

I didn't reply. I closed the door behind me, swept up her sinuous, yielding form into my arms, and carried her through the hallway to the darkened room beyond.

NINETEEN

I checked the notice-board after breakfast the following morning and discovered that Trevor Mason, the flight lieutenant in charge of No.1437 flight, would arrive at 1100 hrs to brief those of us who would be joining his team for the trip west. At the appointed session, Trevor advised us that we would proceed west along the same track and through the same towns that the Eighth Army had already cleared of enemy forces and stragglers. We would take an auxiliary bomb disposal crew with us to double-check that booby traps and all other explosive hazards had been cleared from the aircraft and airfields en route. Another clean-up team would follow on behind our own team, to clear up as much general debris as possible from the landing areas, in preparation for our own squadrons to make use of them. As an additional function, we were to conduct sorties to local communities, distributing whatever food and other supplies we could spare, to help some of the more deprived families survive the widespread destruction of their homes and their farms that the warring armies had, through the years, thrust upon them so indiscriminately.

"Oh, and one other thing," Trevor added at the conclusion of the session,

231

"Departure date has been delayed for a week, so we won't be leaving until December 29."

That meant I had three weeks to make all necessary preparations and assemble our own supplies—and, when possible, see Gabriella again. I determined to make the most of the opportunity. During those three weeks, I saw Gabriella on four more occasions. We made every minute count, making love with abandon whenever we were alone; getting to know each other in the course of long discussions, while dining at her favorite restaurants; in the daytime walking the pathways of her favorite parks and places of interest in the city. Once, we went back to the beach where we'd first met, but despite the absence of those ominous black balls atop the tall poles, I chose not to swim again. We sat on the beach, sunning ourselves and exploring each other's personalities and idiosyncrasies.

We didn't go to a theatre or show of any kind. For us, Gabriella asserted, there wasn't time for that kind of sharing. It would not help us get to know each other and explore each other's lives and hopes and fears. Our romance was an interlude, she said, a cameo on the stage of our lives, that each of us could later revisit in our private hours. It would forever be hers and mine alone, to remember and relive as the mood would take us.

On the third of those heady days together, we took the train to Cairo to visit her mother, Alicia. An attractive and gracious woman, she entertained us with reminiscences of her days as a noted opera singer.

"I would cook for you," she said with an attractive lilting accent, "but tonight, I do not 'ave the, 'ow do you say, ingredigents?—and this is not a good hour to be shopping."

She laughed." But I 'ave an idea; a good one, I tink. We can go to Tommy's Bar. It is only two or tree streets away, and we can 'ave some good English food—roast biff, or steck and kidney pie." She glanced at me to see my reaction.

"And if you like to 'ave sweets, they 'ave the best baklava in all of this City."

The food at Tommy's bar was everything Alicia had claimed for it, and I enjoyed my evening with mother and daughter, marveling at their zest for life and the evident determination of both of them to live in the moment. By the time the famous baklava appeared on our dessert plates, the wine was beginning to have its influence on all three of us. Alicia, now quite playful, looked into my eyes, and then at Gabriella's. She raised her glass and indicated that we should raise ours, too.

"Let us make a toast to love," She said. "I 'ave not before seen my daughter so 'appy."

On the fourth and last day of our romance, a briefing session occupied my morning, so I did not get to ring Gabriella's doorbell until mid-afternoon. The expression in her eyes as I presented her with an oversized bunch of exotic, multi-colored flowers, set angels singing in my heart. She'd prepared well for the occasion, shopping for the makings of our last meal together. We went over the menu: Prosciutto and melon for appetizer, a colorful antipasto for salad, and lobster ravioli for the main

233

course. I had brought red and white wine and a fine brand of Grappa to complete the feast, but as things turned out, we ate and drank very little of it.

We made love slowly and tenderly, as if we wanted this last union to serve as a summation of all our previous lovemaking, an acme of all the intimacies we'd shared in the few weeks we'd known each other. And for the first time, as I caressed her, and buried myself in the wonders of her womanhood, it was Gabriella in my arms, not Verna.

Later, as we were once more picking our way through some of the delicacies that we'd left on the table, Gabri turned to me again and took my hands in hers.

"It was so wonderful, Howard, so very special, this time."

"Was it very different from other times, Gabri?"

"It was for me, Howard. At the height of your passion, the words 'Oh, Gabriella, oh my darling.' burst out of you in a flood of feeling." She cupped my face in her hands. "But until today, the name that always came so readily to your lips, was not Gabriella, it was Verna."

"No, don't speak now." She pressed two fingers to my lips as I was about to say something— to beg her forgiveness and somehow atone for the hurt I must have inflicted on her.

"Don't spoil my little success, Howard. I know now, that I've helped you deal with the ache in your heart, by helping you reserve a little corner of it for me. It will be Gabriella, not just another pretty conquest, that you will think of whenever you reminisce about these joyous days we've had together."

She removed her fingers from my lips. "And what we've shared will stay with you as it will stay with me. It will be worth remembering."

I cast about for something to say, but there was nothing. She was right as she had always been right. Our brief time together had helped me more than she knew, and it did not trespass on my love for Verna, or on what I would always feel for her.

"What do you plan to do with your life, Gabriella?" I asked her.

"I think I want to paint." She said. "I'm good at that."

"Can I see something you've done?"

"No, my darling Howard, I'm not that good yet. I'll send you one of my paintings when I've done something I like well enough," she said. "I won't include a message with it. It will speak for itself. It will tell you that you are still tucked away safely in a corner of my heart."

TWENTY

December 1942

We made rapid progress in our journey west. The cleaning up of the airfields at Benghazi and Tobruk were the only en-route tasks assigned to us before proceeding to the Castel Benito Airport in Tripolitania.

There wasn't a lot left to inspect in Benghazi and Tobruk. The relics of German, Italian, and British aircraft were so scattered that they didn't appear to be interesting subjects for study, and therefore, hardly worth the planting of booby-traps.

Our bomb-disposal experts nonetheless conducted thorough examinations of every corner and every remaining piece of scrap metal at those historic battle sites.

At Castel Benito airfield in Tripoli, the scene was somewhat different. Here, the enemy had not had time to destroy the many machines that were scattered around the airfield, but as we later discovered, they hadn't had enough time either, to set booby traps. We didn't find any, and were quickly able to declare the field safe for others to crawl over the relics of the enemy occupation, and learn what they might about their aeronautical technology.

Time now to turn our attention to the good-will missions we'd been instructed to pursue while awaiting orders to return to the Nile delta. We lost no time in assuming the roles of good-will ambassadors— to reassure the Tripolitanian people that we were there to help them and not to further deplete their already minimal supplies of the essentials in life. To this end, I instructed my team to load our Jeep with all kinds of canned foods—sausages, McConnakie's Meat and Vegetables, baked beans, cases of Brooke-Bond's tea and the like and, each day for several days, we set out on tours of the farms in the area, sometimes ranging as far as twenty miles from Castel Benito itself. The effort was as rewarding as we could have hoped, and the hospitality we received in return was heartwarming.

Our experience on the last day of our mission was typical. At about 11 am on that day, we drove through the gates of a farm on the outskirts of the village of Carpi about ten miles south-west of Castel Benito.

As we approached the homestead, I greeted a lean and leathery faced person who was clearly interested in the approaching military people.

"Buon Giorno, Signore."

He eyed me suspiciously, and walked slowly toward us, but did not immediately reply. I grabbed a tin of Heinz baked beans, and another of Spam, and handed them to him. Still expressionless, he spoke for the first time. "Inglesi?" he asked.

"Si, Signore," I replied, and he nodded his head, now somewhat more relaxed. He turned on his heel and made his way back to the farm-house, calling to us over his shoulder. "Aspetti, aspetti," before disappearing through the front entrance.

In a short while, the farmhouse door opened again and a somewhat older man appeared with a buxom, shawl-draped woman at his side. After inspecting us and our jeep for a minute or so, they stepped forward and offered their hands in greeting.

"Benvenuto signore," the man said. "Che cosa volare."

"We have food," I replied somewhat awkwardly, while I grabbed one or two more cans of the supplies we'd brought with us. "Please take these." I thrust them into his hands. He examined them and read the labels.

"Grazie Signore, Eo sono Alberto e questo e mio Moglie."

I could feel the easing of their suspicions and concerns. A few minutes later, Alberto invited us into their farmhouse and introduced us to their attractive teen-aged daughter who spoke some halting English. "My name is Angela, she said, and my parents would like you to stay for some tea."

We offered our thanks and took seats around a small table on which a spotlessly clean red and white tablecloth had just been placed in our honor. In a short while, Alberto took a small, long-handled canister of boiling water from the top of their wood-fired stove and, with some ceremony, poured its contents into another similar container in which a quantity of dry tea leaves had been placed.

As he placed the mix back on the stove to boil up again, he added several tea-spoonsful of sugar. Then, when the container began steaming again, he removed it from the stove-top and poured the steaming liquid back into its original container. When he had done so, he held up the now full container and brought it closer to me so that I could examine its pewter-like appearance. "Cannaker," he said, thrusting it a little closer to me for emphasis. "esta un cannaker." He poured several more spoons of sugar into the brew and placed it back on the stove to re-boil. A minute or so later, he poured the hot liquid back into its original container, added yet more sugar and placed it back on the stove to re-boil. This periodic pouring back and forth between the two containers, with the re-boiling and addition of more sugar each time, continued until the hot tea had assumed a very dark treacle consistency.

Alberto then poured the resulting beverage into several demi-tasse sized cups and handed one to each of us. He beamed as he informed us that this was true 'Arab' tea.

Strangely, the taste and texture of the brew reminded me of the Turkish 'moccha' that I'd found so popular in Cairo and Alexandria, except, of course, that it was much sweeter.

We thanked Alberto and his family for their hospitality, and after placing a further variety of our canned goods on his table, we took our leave and continued on our rounds. As we drove down the rutted track to the roadway, our cockney driver muttered,

"Gawd, what we do for England!"

The order we'd been expecting, awaited us on our return to the Castel Benito air-field. The necessary personnel had arrived to operate the airport for allied planes, and the flying members of our bomb-disposal team, myself included, were to standby for a flight back to Cairo.

I turned to my 55 Squadron counterpart, Trevor, who'd spent the last several days leading his own separate party on good-will missions.

"So what shall we do to celebrate our last night in Tripoli, Trev?"

"Go out on a bender and celebrate with the locals," He replied smartly.

"What do you mean, exactly?"

"Let's go find one of those underground stores of Chianti and make merry."

"Oh, I know where there's one of those only a mile or two from here," I told him.

"Wizard, let's do it."

In the early evening we made our way to a village a few miles south of the city. As the sun began to sink in a blood-red sky, we located a clearing where several local farmers were gathered around a polished marble edifice, the center of which was carved in the shape of a lion's head, its noble mane etched into the stonework above.

Its mouth gaped wide open and its tongue projected enough to serve as a spout from which red wine flowed continuously into a receptacle below. A farmer wearing a beige galabia moved forward and held an earthenware chatty in the path of the stream until it was full of the dark red liquid.

We sat on a nearby rough wooden bench and watched as other local residents stepped forward and, in their turn, held their various containers under the lion's mouth.

A dark-haired boy, probably in his early teens, seemed to be following our interest in the proceedings. He strolled over to us.

"Why don't you have some wine, signore," he said with a musical English accent. "It belongs to the local farms and there is plenty. I will get you a container and something to drink from."

He walked away toward one of the tables before we could comment, and in moments he was back again with two earthenware mugs and a chatty like the ones we'd seen the farmers use for their supplies.

"Go," he said, "Take." We took the chatty from him and thanked him.

"What's your name?"

"I am Alberto. I will wait for you."

"Would you like to get it for us?" I ventured.

"No. It is bad luck."

We walked over to the lion's head and filled our container.

Gathering once more at our table, we drank and talked with Alberto.

"How is it that anyone can come here and help themselves to the wine?" I asked.

"No, signore, that is not the case. The wine belongs to the farmers who contribute their supplies, and everyone knows who they are. The people are honest and they don't trespass."

"What about all the military?"

Alberto laughed. "They did that once. They began to take lots of it. Then, after a while, many of them came down with a mysterious illness. Soon everybody knew that our wine was not fit for Europeans, so we didn't have to poison it anymore."

We chuckled at their resourcefulness.

"And how does the system work, Alberto?"

"Well, grape growers can't afford to have their own winery, so they band together into local associations for that, and they all get their share of the wine according to the grapes they contribute. We store it underground because it keeps better that way and holds a better temperature." He paused.

"And it's pumped up all the time and re-circulated through filters as it goes back down, so it's always pure."

"It's an interesting story, Alberto. You are being very generous with us. I would have thought you would not want to have anything to do with military people again, after what you've told us."

"Word spreads fast, Signore. You are giving us food, everything you can spare, so you can help yourself to as much wine as you like."

TWENTY ONE

No. 22 Personnel Transit Center

July1943 —January1945

Twenty-two PTC (Personnel Training Center) at Heliopolis, near Cairo, served as a combined transit center, training school, and central airfield for the RAF, and since the chief instructor had recently been posted elsewhere, I'd been appointed as his replacement.

My task was to hone the navigation and communication skills of aircrew members passing through, and occupy them profitably for whatever time they might be stationed there while awaiting transfer to operational squadrons. Aircrew members arrived at this center from anywhere in the Middle-East Command, or directly from the UK. From this center, they would be posted to whichever squadrons might need replacements for crews lost in battle, or to replace those posted for rest periods.

I sensed that this would be my last job in this arena until the time would come for my return to the UK, so I did my best to make a worthwhile contribution.

The immense resources of the Allied war machine were by this time growing faster than the rate at which they could be used. In the Middle-East at least, there began to be a surplus, and this fact was made evident by the rate that the number of personnel arriving at 22 PTC gradually exceeded postings away from the center.

Many would, after all their preparation for service in the Middle East, find themselves repatriated to the United Kingdom without having seen a day of action, and I realized well enough that my own time for that posting was also drawing near. There was simply nothing more for aircrews to do in this once teeming war-zone, and those that remained were rapidly becoming obsolescent.

D-Day had come and gone, and it was increasingly evident that even when our postings home would take effect, there would, for many of us, no longer be jobs to do, even in Britain. We were simply marking time.

Much as I tried to occupy myself with the task of preparing an increasing number of airmen for a decreasing number of operational functions and postings, it was not enough.

I asked the Australian Station Commander, S\Ldr Leon Ames what one was supposed to do with one's free time besides drinking and sight-seeing.

"It's obvious, sir, that I'm going to have less and less to do here while I'm awaiting my own posting back to England. I need to be occupied."

"I don't know why you restless young men have to be always on the go," he said.

"But if you do need activity, why don't you try the Heliopolis Sporting Club? It's only a couple of miles away, and there's a huge swimming pool there and a bunch of tennis courts. When station transport isn't available, there's a regular bus service that stops a few yards from our main gate." He stared at me thoughtfully. "You know Layton, it surprises me that in all the months you've been here, you don't already know all this."

He shook his head in puzzlement. "I think you've been burying yourself here. Better get out a bit and take a break from all those maps and charts."

The station commander's words came back to me as I lounged in a gaily striped deck-chair at the side of the Heliopolis Club pool. He was right. I had, indeed, been burying myself. I'd been afraid to get in touch with Gabriella, somehow convinced that our time together had been fated to be just a cameo in our lives that would end in disappointment for both of us if we tried to prolong it.

Marry her? No, I could not for one moment imagine the exotic Gabriella involved with daily life in my home country, weathering the English winters and the fog and drizzle of those special days in autumn and spring, taking the bus to Broadgate and shopping at Marks and Spencer's and Boots The Chemist, or taking a walk through the woods, clad in tweeds and galoshes to navigate puddles and dampness of a kind so endearing to the British, so unknown to Egyptians.

No, Gabri was not for that kind of life. She was an exotic flower, born in and for the kind of exotic environment offered by the two cities in which she'd been raised. To transplant her to so different an environment as she would find in dear old England, would be akin to trying to raise orchids where only daffodils were supposed to thrive. Gabriella was for me a precious interlude in my life, a life-line when I most needed one. I would always be grateful to her for that, but that was what our time together must always be, in her heart and in mine—an interlude. As my visits to the Heliopolis Club became a regular part of my weekly curriculum, the swimming and sunning, and the socializing, helped to ease the emptiness in my life, and my grieving for Verna.

In the course of my fourth visit, my after-swim sunbathing in a pool-side deck-chair was interrupted by a thorough drenching. Someone had just been thrown into the deep end close to my chosen corner, and I lay directly in the path of the resulting watery fall-out.

A bronzed, well built, fine-looking fellow appeared out of nowhere.

"Sorry old chap. Frank Snapes at your service. I didn't mean to drench you, but I had to show that Hussie who's boss. She's been trying to dunk me all afternoon. He grinned as the 'Hussie' he was referring to, swam over to where I was sitting.

"Some gentleman," she called after him as she hauled herself out of the water. "I'll get you yet." Then she turned her dark brown eyes toward me and smiled radiantly.

"As you saw, it wasn't my fault that I got you all soaked, but I apologize just the same."

I got to my feet and offered my hand. "You can drench me as often as you like, if I can get a smile like that each time," I told her.

"I'm Laura," she said, taking my hand in hers "Glad to meet you."

"Delighted to meet you, too," I replied, "My name's Howard."

I looked around. "Where did your boy-friend go?"

She laughed. "He's my sister's boyfriend. I'll introduce you to her if you'd like."

We strolled down to the end of the pool to the veranda at the side of the club house.

"There they are," Laura said, pointing to one of the tables that lined the outside wall.

As we walked over, Frank rose and motioned us to be seated. Laura began the introductions.

"Howard, I'd like you to meet my sister, André."

Looking across the table, I saw a teenaged girl, her dark hair crowning a lovely, lightly tanned face, devoid of any trace of makeup. The smile she gave me as she gestured for me to be seated was the most serene and angelic I had ever seen, but as we all conversed, I learned from her animated gestures that she lacked the power of speech and did not hear very well either. Mostly, André relied on lip-reading to keep abreast of the conversation.

We sat quietly, enjoying each other's company and sipping mint juleps. It was hard to imagine that there was still a war on. Frank, a ferry pilot, at present carrying men and machines to and from the UK, told us of his schedule for departure the following day, and I imagined myself sneaking on board, so I could pay Verna a surprise visit and persuade her to give me another chance.

As I pondered the matter, a more practical plan occurred to me. I should find out when Frank's subsequent departure would occur to give myself time to apply to my commanding officer for two or three week's leave so my absence would be legal. I turned it over and over in my mind.

"Frank," I asked. "How often do you do these trips— back and forth to the UK, I mean?"

"Oh, about once a month on average," He grinned, knowingly. "Could it be that you're thinking of coming along some time?"

"Actually, something like that did cross my mind. Would that be a problem if I got some leave?"

"Well, the timing of the return journey is never cast in concrete, and that could give you problems with your C/O. Other than that, I would have no trouble taking you along."

Frank seemed to be considering further possibilities.

"I shall be landing here again in another three or four weeks on my way from Aden to the UK. There would probably be room for you on that flight."

"Aden? I was stationed there. You must be bringing some of the chaps who took over from our outfit. What a hell-hole that was."

"Yes and it still is," he said, "but about your ride back home, let me tell you what I can do. As soon as I know the date of my flight back here again, I'll call you at your base or send you a signal through the regular channels. It can't be more than three weeks."

As I scribbled the contact information for him, I noticed André gesturing wildly. Laura interpreted her sign language for us.

"André is saying that what Frank does is just as dangerous as bombing or combat flying. Frank got himself shot at on his way here last time."

André made several signs again and Laura interpreted.

"I hope you say your prayers every night without fail."

"Can't do that," Frank replied. "I'm an agnostic."

"Be reasonable Frank," Laura said. "You've got to have faith in someone or something when you're facing danger. What if you got hit badly and you had to bail out? What if you found yourself in the sea with no help anywhere around? What would you think of then?"

Frank smiled. "I'd think of Frank Snapes in the water, and I'd concentrate on what I'd better try to do about that."

André turned to me and formed the words with her mouth and with gestures.

"Howard, please talk to him."

I smiled at her ruefully. "I can't do that, André. My own views are very close to Frank's. I used to think I was an agnostic, too, but now I've changed a bit."

"You mean you believe in God now?"

"That's right, André. I don't think anyone can consider nature as a whole, or look at the infinity of the stars through a telescope, or even consider the miracle of birth, without believing in a higher power than we poor mortals." André and Laura both reacted at the same time.

"So why do you say that your views are very close to Frank's?"

"Because mine is a very different kind of god from the one you all believe in."

"How so?" Laura questioned.

"I think of my God as a kind of Mother Nature, the creator of all things, from the vastness of space to the smallest blade of grass, but my god is not compassionate. She does not intervene to prevent a tragedy, or rescue anyone or anything from harm or misery. If that were not so, innocent children would not be born with crippling defects, while others are perfectly formed. Cancer would not afflict a kindly man or woman, while evil souls live in health. A destructive fire would not burn the flesh off a saintly man's face, while the arsonist who set it, escapes scot-free."

"By what strange manipulations of ordinary reason do we persuade ourselves that God favors one creature over another; that the families who perished in a flood were more sinful or more deserving of death than those who were rescued? Is the deer that escapes the predator's teeth more deserving than the one that is felled? Is there any evidence whatever that anyone's fate is other than randomly ordained?"

I know I'm talking too much, but one thing seems very clear to me: God is fair in her choice of who shall suffer or who shall not, solely because she does not choose at all."

"So you are against religion?" Laura asked.

"No, no, not at all. I respect all conventional religions equally. They advocate good principles for people to live by. They encourage people to help each other, and that in the end is the core of my own religious beliefs. I am like Abou Ben Adhem, who, when challenged by the angel about his belief in God, replied: 'Put me down as one who loves his fellow men.'"

I looked around at my attentive audience.

"I know I'm on my soap box again but I might as well finish what I've started.

I really do believe that religion is an important influence in people's lives, but I'm sure that God, whoever She may be, or whatever mankind may wish to name her, doesn't care which of the various religions of this world is used as the pathway to belief in her ultimate power over all of us."

Another hour of spirited conversation passed. Frank and André took their leave, and for reasons of chivalry, I offered to walk Laura home.

Not knowing what was expected of me as we reached the entrance to her home in a condominium complex in the center of Heliopolis, I pulled her to me and kissed her gently on her cheek.

"Goodnight Laura, Good night."

In the bus on the way back to 22 PTC, I muttered to myself about my stupidities.

'I'd better steer clear of that club for a while. Otherwise, I'll just get myself embroiled in another romance. And it's going to end up the same way. We'll get emotionally involved and it will only lead to heartbreak. Laura is another exotic flower like Gabriella, and she would wither away and die in a place like England. No, it mustn't happen.'

I stayed away and buried myself in the world of navigation instruction again. I intensified the curriculum and introduced more operational examples of navigation challenges in the Middle-East environment, but it could not go on forever. Our worthy Australian Station Commander was watching me, and he insisted that I get off the station once in a while.

Three weeks had slipped by since our meeting at the club, but I had not had the promised word from Frank about his return date.

Once every week thereafter, I poked my nose into the sporting club again, chiefly to look for André, and to ask her whether she'd heard anything from Frank, but on my first three visits, I saw no sign of André or her sister or Frank.

On the fourth week, I fared better.

I caught sight of André almost immediately, exercising her diving skills. I sat at the poolside watching her graceful performance until she glanced in my direction and swam over to the side close to where I was sitting. She looked up at me and made signs that she and Laura had wondered why I'd stayed away, and I tried to explain that I'd been deeply involved with my instructional obligations, but that I had dropped into the club once a week for the last several weeks and had not seen them.

André climbed out and sat on the edge of the pool next to me, dangling her feet and swinging her legs back and forth in the water. She seemed pensive.

Forgetting her hearing impairment, I asked, "Have you heard from Frank, André?"

She looked up at me with a troubled expression, shaping words with her mouth and gestures.

"What did you say?"

I tried to make it easy for her to read my lips "I was wondering whether you'd heard from Frank," I mouthed.

She looked away and was silent for a long moment. Then she turned and looked up at me again, eyes brimming. She shook her head slowly from side to side as she mouthed the word "No." She gestured again and explained that until his last visit, she had always had a letter from Frank every week and occasional phone calls as well. This time there'd been nothing since he'd left, and that was now seven weeks ago. I felt the old ache in the pit of my stomach, and I put my arm around her. As I sat there with André, patting her shoulder to comfort her, I ached for both of us.

I went on patting her gently, my mind a million miles away, while something inside me crumbled and died.

I met Elsie, a matronly soul who said she was a friend of Laura's, and that Laura had been asking about me. A few days later, I met Laura at the club again and apologized for my absence, and soon after that, we were going places together. Lunches in town; a visit to the pyramids; sight-seeing in the centre of Cairo.

I knew I was falling into the trap again, so I decided to tell her I would be going away and would not be back for some months. One evening, as I was saying goodnight to her on her doorstep, I broached the subject.

"Laura," I said, "I have to go away for a while."

"Yes, yes," she replied, "I knew that was bound to happen. That's why I didn't tell you that my father has been very angry with me for seeing you." Her deep brown eyes flashed rebelliously. "All these weeks I've been seeing you, it has been without my father's knowledge or consent." She stamped her small feet and clenched her fists. "He threatened to turn me out of the house if I continued to associate with you at all."

"But why is that?" I asked, surprised by this turn of events.

"Well, in case you didn't know, we are Jewish, and my father is adamant that I shall not get involved with anyone who is not of our faith."

Laura's revelation changed everything. Her father's objection affected me as a red flag might affect a bull. I was no longer concerned about the wisdom of continuing to see Laura, or whether or not I had or would develop serious intentions about her. No, the rules had changed now. Her father had presented me with a challenge that I was not in a mood to ignore. If his primary purpose had been to encourage a suitor for his daughter, he could not have done better than to issue the edict I had just been made aware of.

I turned it over in my mind. As an agnostic, it really made no difference to me at all whether I was categorized as Jew or Christian. They were both fine, serious faiths and their differences in outlook seemed trivial to me. And in any case, what did I care about religion, or love or anything else for that matter? Nothing mattered to me any more. Laura was a lovely girl. If I could somehow make her happy, that would be better than wasting my life pining endlessly for a girl I'd lost.

I made up my mind. I would become a Jew.

"Laura," I said. "I shall not see you for a while, but you can tell your father that the next time I meet you, I will go with you to meet him, present myself as a Jew and ask him for your hand in marriage.

That night, alone in my quarters, away from Laura and everyone else, I did some soul searching. Were my agnostic convictions totally genuine? Did I really believe what I so readily espoused? Were all the accepted religions of the world of equal significance to me? Most importantly, could I so readily abandon the Christian Methodist faith that I'd grown up with? Did I really have the courage of my convictions?

I found that I did.

I consulted the Rabbi of the Heliopolis synagogue, who was glad to prepare a course of instruction for me, and help me understand the Talmud and the elements of the Jewish Doctrine. Following the early weeks of instruction, the rabbi advised me that I would have to be circumcised. I applied to the RAF authorities for permission to proceed with this ritual, and, in due course, I was admitted into the RAF military hospital in Cairo.

No one who has not actually experienced the agonies of circumcision as an adult can imagine what excruciating pain this entailed. It was not so much the operation itself that was so punishing, it was the means by which I was anesthetized for the procedure and the recovery there-from, that was so difficult to bear. A series of lumbar injections left me writhing in agony, and I began to wonder what aberrations of rational thinking had conspired to launch me into this folly. There were times when I felt that death would be preferable to the pain that dominated my waking day and made it impossible for me to sleep at night.

In a little more than a week it was over. At the next conference with the Rabbi, the name of Dahud (David) was conferred upon me. I was now a Jew, and what is more, as the Rabbi advised me, I now knew more about Jewish principles and practices than most who were born into that faith.

"You should know, Dahud," the Rabbi told me one day, "that in our society, it is the custom for the bride to bring a dowry to her husband. After the wedding, Laura's father will make provision for this. It will be a substantial sum, but it is our way of sending the couple happily on their way and ensuring that they will have a good start in their blessed journey together. However, it is also understood that if the marriage fails and the daughter is returned to her parents' home, you will repay her father twice the amount of his original gift, and you will be asked to sign a document, signifying your acceptance of that arrangement and obligation." The Rabbi smiled and patted my hand. "But of course, since you've been through so much to prove your love for your betrothed, it will never come to that, will it?"

Laura's family accepted me whole-heartedly and there followed a period of visits to her home, meeting her parents, Ezra and Allegra, her other sisters Raymonde and little Jessie, and her brothers Moni and Mickey. I also got to know Ándre a little better, and in the few short weeks of my visits to the Chalom apartment, I began to gain an understanding of the sign language on which she relied so heavily.

Ezra, especially, welcomed my company. Whenever I was free to visit his home, he liked to rest his large, portly frame in an ancient-looking wicker armchair by the French windows and drink a sundowner with me before dinner.

"'Oward, is good, this drink," he told me on my first visit. "Good for digestion; good before eating." The cocktail consisted of iced water to which had been added a generous portion of Zibib and a sprig of mint. I found the flavor of the milky aniseed beverage very pleasant.

Allegra, dark, handsome, full figured, and dressed in a flowing black lace gown, bustled in from the kitchen, carrying several small glass dishes. A maid followed, bearing a large bowl of some sort of appetizer which she placed on the dining-room table.

"I hope you will like this, 'oward," Allegra said. "It is a mixture of sliced cucumber, chopped ice, yogurt and mint. Where I come from in Syria," she said, "it is called leben-ze-bahdi, and we have it with our cocktails."

She handed me one of the dishes. "Take," she said, "It will give you good appetite."

I found the combination of flavors refreshing, and asked if I could have the recipe.

"You must not worry about that," she said, laughing, "Laura knows 'ow to make it."

We chatted at length on those occasions, and I learned something of Ezra's background and how he'd made his fortune trading cotton in Haiti. In turn, I told him about my own family and what it had been like growing up in England with my brother and mother. On the eve of our wedding, Ezra took me aside.

" 'Oward," he said, "The Rabbi, I think, told you about our custom to give newly married couples a dowry, and I want you to know that I gave a thousand pounds to Laura for that purpose several weeks ago to get you both off to a good start."

A thousand pounds! More than twice my annual pay! I thanked him profusely for his generosity.

In the ensuing weeks, Laura occupied herself with visits to her dress-maker and shoemaker, gradually accumulating a trousseau of such magnitude and splendor that I began to wonder how we would be able to get it all safely to England. At any rate, I marveled at her father's generosity for footing the bill for such an extensive wardrobe. It was not until I took my leave of both parents for the last time, that Ezra motioned me to join him on the veranda, where we could talk privately.

" 'Oward," he said, shaking his head from side to side in a gesture of benevolent disapproval, "I think I must tell you that I made a big mistake in giving your dowry to Laura. She has used up every penny of it for her trousseau."

Allegra, I learned, had always given Laura and her siblings everything that their hearts might desire, and Ezra had long since abandoned his attempts to counter her indulgences in this area, so one could not blame any of her children for knowing nothing of the value of money, nor of the difficulties encountered when there was not enough of it to go around.

I shrugged my shoulders. If Laura didn't know how to work with a budget, I would just have to teach her.

On August 2nd, 1944, in the principal synagogue of Cairo, with all her family present and rejoicing, Laura and I were married. We honeymooned at Mena House in the shadow of the Great Pyramids, and on January 15th 1945, we sailed for England.

TWENTY TWO

England, 1945-51

Flying through the mists over the Irish Sea, looking for lighthouses and radio beacons, may not have made the top of the list of my favorite things to do with my time, but that's where I found myself, night after night following the couple of weeks leave at home after my return to England.

By this time, with the end in sight, huge armadas of heavy bombers were taking to the skies every night, pounding the enemy's great cities, airfields, dams, and bridges to hasten that end. To help these swarms of allied aircraft identify their targets, fast, light, unarmed, twin-engine aircraft known as 'Pathfinders' preceded the bombers to their destinations, and after making careful identification, dropped flares that would illuminate the entire target areas. These pathfinders were the 'Mosquitoes' which, by virtue of their light-weight balsawood construction, could out-fly most other aircraft in the sky.

My own night-flying course of instruction was intended to prepare me for navigation duties in those

Pathfinder aircraft. By the time I'd completed the training, however, the demand for Mosquito crews had diminished to the point where no further use of my flying services was foreseen. Like countless numbers of my fellow airmen, I was re-allocated to ground-based duties, then sent home on leave while awaiting posting.

Coventry, my home town, proved unrecognizable. Corrugated iron Nissen huts and other temporary structures occupied the places on Hartford and Smithford streets where Woolworths and Marks and Spencer's had once stood, and Corporation Street, our most modern achievement in 1939, had been totally wiped out. I walked to the place where I grew up, but Cope Street no longer existed. All that remained were the curbstones at the top end where High Street led the way to the Cathedral, now a shattered ruin. I found it difficult to navigate my way around Jordon Well and Gosford Street. Halford's, where in the past I had bought my cycling accessories, and Patricks Milinary Store on the opposite side of the street, were both more or less undamaged, but the Council House and the area around it had been completely replaced by modern-looking equivalents. I took the bus home to the Coventry suburb of Stoke, and walked down Crescent Avenue to my home in Emscote Road. The solid rows of semi-detached houses hadn't changed much since I'd left four and a half years earlier. A bit shabbier, perhaps, but otherwise they remained their same gray, solid, respectable selves. Emscote Road was home, and I was thankful that as improbable an outcome as it had seemed, fate had decreed that I would return unscathed to see it again.

Despite my mother's instinctive distrust of all things and people not made or born in England, she hit it off with Laura from the day they met, and set about doing everything she could to make her feel at home. She taught Laura how to cook some of the most popular English meals; roast beef with Yorkshire pudding, steak and kidney pie. She coached her in the art of preparing rack of lamb so that it would be moist and juicy. In the mornings, Laura was quickly introduced to traditional English breakfasts of bacon or sausage and eggs, with my favorite addition; tomato chunks fried 'til the edges of the skins burned and curled.

Despite the fact that cooking had never been Laura's strong suit, she, in turn, introduced mother to mousaka and fûl, and other popular Mediterranian dishes she'd grown up with, and much to my surprise and delight, mother seemed to enjoy them all.

When, by mid-summer, my mother learned that the wheels were already in motion to make her a grandmother by the following spring, she could not have been happier; and when, in the late spring of the following year, a baby girl graced us with her tiny wrinkled presence, mother wept with joy.

I lost no time in catching up with my pre-war friends, among them, older, studious, professorial, Roy Flowers. One April afternoon I walked up to Crescent Avenue and across the Binley Road to Roy's home. We drank tea laced with rum and talked about what we intended to do with our lives.

"What now, Roy?" I asked him.

"Oh, I don't know, Howard. I'll probably go back to the labs at the GEC. It's interesting work and I've got some pretty good seniority. What about you, Howard, what will you do?"

I pondered his question for several moments.

"I'm thinking seriously about staying in the service," I replied. "If I don't do that, there are a couple of alternatives I've been thinking about. I've always longed to fly so I might explore possibilities in that direction. The trouble is that there are countless well trained pilots already available for the airlines to gobble up, so my chances for being considered would be pretty slim." I paused.

"Airlines don't expect to have to train pilots from scratch, so I might have to put off any moves in that direction until I can afford to pay for training myself."

"Then it looks like staying in the service might be a good bet for you my friend," Roy mused.

"Well, there are at least two other possibilities. Between all the technical training I had before the war, and the signals and radar training and experience I've had in the service, I could get a job in electrical or radio engineering or even in technical sales. That might well be the best way for me to go, Roy."

He nodded his head. "I know it's a bit early for alcohol, but what about a glass of sherry? We'll drink to the future and whatever it holds."

"Thanks, Roy. I still have a bit of time before I have to take Laura shopping."

I sat there reminiscing while Roy busied himself getting sherry glasses from the sideboard and dispensing Dry Fly from a bottle on the counter.

"And what's the other possibility you mentioned," he asked as he brought two glasses of the pale gold liquor over to the small table in front of us.

"Well, there is one other thing that keeps nagging at me, Roy."

"What's that, my friend," he said as he handed me one of the glasses.

"I could go on the stage."

Roy stared at me.

"You're not serious, Howard." More a statement than a question.

"Yes I am, Roy."

I considered how best I could answer. Roy, staunch, serious, always solicitous, deserved an honest answer.

"If you're interested, I'll tell you about that, Roy," I said.

He studied my face and nodded slowly. "This I have to hear."

I took a sip of my sherry and told him the story of my childhood and the re-awakening of my longing to be on the stage when Verna and I had seen 'Arsenic and Old Lace' together. Even as I said the words again, I felt the excitement I'd known when I'd poured it all out to Verna for the first time.

"There's another thing, too, that has helped to keep that nagging ambition alive all this time. It's something I've never told anyone."

Roy sat there, impassive, letting me know that I could continue and tell him the rest of my story or not, as I felt inclined.

"In the course of my visits to the Heliopolis sporting club, I met two Australian ladies on the tennis courts. They invited me to join a foursome with the two of them and another friend. After we'd been playing together a few times, they told me that they were news people and that they were friendly with a chap from MGM Studios who was on the lookout for talent for his organization. His name was Albert Kraus, or something like that, and he was currently in Jerusalem for some special function or other. These ladies had decided that I had the kind of looks and personality that would interest their friend and they were adamant that I should get on a plane and go visit him. They would fix up the interview, they said. The following week they told me that they had talked with Kraus and that he was looking forward to my visit. I knew it would be easy to arrange a ride in an RAF dispatch plane, because I'd done the same thing a year before when I'd been sent up to Lady McMichael's Rest home in Jerusalem to get myself cured of Sinusitis. A date was set, but when I learned that my longed for visit to plead with Verna had fallen through, I lost interest in everything and everyone, including Albert Kraus, so the meeting never took place and I never learned what might have come of it."

When I'd finished, I grinned and looked across at Roy.

"Now you know all my secrets."

He sat there in a kind of reverie for a while, his dark brow furrowed and his head nodding very slightly up and down. Then he looked up at me again.

"For a man with a wife and child, the stage is a pretty uncertain life isn't it?"

"Well, I feel pretty uncertain about everything these days, Roy. Perhaps it's because in the end, that ship you helped me find plans for, didn't serve the purpose that I'd hoped."

"I'm really sorry old friend," he said.

I walked back slowly along Pembroke to its intersection with Binley Road.

As I looked right and left for a way to dodge the traffic, I saw her. Verna, riding her bicycle on her way home from work at the GEC, had just come around the corner of Crescent Avenue onto Binley road, right where I was crossing. As her cycle approached the spot opposite where I was standing, I stared at her, speechless. She glanced in my direction, and our eyes met and held for one long moment. Then she tossed her lovely head and rode on.

"Verna!" I yelled. "Vernaaa!" I ran after her as fast
as I could, oblivious to the passing bikes and cars, and
the clamor around me. "Vernaaaaaaa!"

I ran and ran, mindless and blinded by road dust and
my own welling tears. An open-topped Morris Minor shot
past me, its driver screaming obscenities as he passed;
motorbikes and bicycles swerved wildly, their riders
shouting for me to get out of their way. I collapsed in the
street, still screaming her name, straining my eyes to
keep her in view and watched her graceful form recede
until, at the bottom of the slope near the Bull's Head
Inn, her beloved silhouette merged with the swelling
traffic flow.

Oh Verna . . . Oh my darling . . .

" Vernaaaaaaaaa . . ."

My God, how stupid could I be? How could I have
imagined that I would be able to live in the same city
with her, knowing that she would forever be out of my
reach?

That same evening, I told Laura that until I could see
where a worthwhile future for us would lie, I would stay
in the RAF, and that would entail moving into married
quarters on an RAF Station.

As I made the announcement, I knew that Laura
would not welcome such a lifestyle. She'd talked of
settling down in a permanent home in Coventry, and had
not expected that I would opt for a life in the service

with its periodic upheavals whenever postings would occur.

She shook her head impatiently when I said the words.

"Howard, what's eating you?" She paced the floor, her high heels tapping stridently. "What is it that makes you seem always so far away—in another world? I just can't reach you. You're always somewhere else and I'm sick of it." Her dark eyes flashed with hurt and indignation.

"I'm sorry Laura. I think the war has affected me in ways I hadn't expected, and I just don't know what I should be aiming at or what career path will offer us the best chances in life together. I'm beginning to wonder whether England is the place for me or for us anymore. It's an endless reminder of the past. It will always be slow to change or to let its citizens make up for the years they've lost in the war." I paused and held her face in my hands.

"People think they can come back after more than four years away and expect to pick up their lives where they left off. The reality is not like that at all. For me, despite the horrors of war and the constant risks involved, the eternal sunshine and openness of the Mediterranean climate changed my outlook. A part of me thrived in that climate and wanted to stay there forever. As for you, since you were born to the Mediterranean sunshine and its blue skies, I was almost sure that the damp and the drizzle of the English weather would be very depressing for you." I sighed and shook my head.

"Instead of that, it is not you, it is I who has become oppressed by the change back to the mists and rain-soaked days and nights I grew up with."

Laura nodded slowly, seemingly doing her best to settle to the idea of a continuing service life. She went back to her seat again. Then, a moment later, she looked up at me questioningly.

"What do you really want, Howard? Would you like me to go back to where I came from, and just admit that this marriage was a mistake?" She paused, gathering strength to express the thought she was struggling with.

"I could do that, you know. My family would welcome me wholeheartedly." She tossed her head. "My mother and father told me that if either you or I should decide that our marriage was a mistake, I would be welcomed back at any time."

I looked at her upturned face as tears escaped and trickled down her cheeks, and much to my amazement, I found I could not take the course she was suggesting. Laura was offering me an opportunity to correct the mindless mistake I'd made. She had opened the door for me to regain my freedom, to pursue my quest to recapture the love of my life; free to beg Verna for her forgiveness, and to prevail in my cause through the sheer force of my longing to be by her side. I realized then, that it could never be. Verna, as precious to me as she was, would from this day forward belong to my past.

Time to grow up; time to accept reality, and time to take some responsibility for my actions as a married man and father. I had to consider what would be best for that trusting little girl who'd come into our lives to give meaning to our union. I was fortunate indeed, and it was high time I set about earning that good fortune.

I took Laura's hand and led her over to our Danish-modern settee.

"Please listen to me Laura," I said. "It may not seem that way to you, but I really do want our marriage to succeed. I know I've been irresponsible and self-centered all my life, but I promise you I'm going to change that." I searched for words to better express what was in my mind.

"Laura, I know it's hard for you to believe, but I want to be a good husband and father. If you can just give me time to work my way through this transition from war to peace, from living each day as if it were my last and packing my kit every night because there might not be a tomorrow; from having no one but myself to care about; to make the switch from all that futility to a life of preparing and planning for a worthwhile future for the three of us; if you can bear with me while I wrestle with that, I promise you I will work at it with everything that's in me." I paused again.

"I can't deny that it will take time, Laura. And I shall surely make mistakes, but somehow, I'm going to find a way for us."

Laura looked up at me again, her indignation subsiding. A long pause. Then she rose and paced the floor once more.

"Alright, I'll do my best, but you'd better make up your mind pretty soon, what you want to do with your life—and mine."

I took an eighteen-month concentrated course in radio communications at the RAF College in Cranwell, followed by two other six-month courses in radar technology. Shortly thereafter, I was appointed Sector Signals Officer for the Eastern Sector of Fighter Command at Horsham St. Faiths, but the daily routine in that capacity showed me quite soon that peace-time military service with all its red-tape would not keep me sufficiently interested and occupied. Within little more than a year of completing my signals training courses, I resigned my commission.

On the last day of my service, the Station Commander called me into his office to wish me well.

"By the way," he said, as he shook my hand. "A signal came in today to say that your pilot's course has finally come through. Pity, isn't it, that it took so long."

I set about studying for a career on the stage. It seemed to me that if I didn't get it out of my system while I was still young enough, I would always wonder what it would have been like, and why I had not had the gumption to go for it while I had the chance. I knew I would blame myself later in life if I didn't. I got myself accepted by the J. Arthur Rank School of Acting at the Connaught Theater in Worthing on the south coast and followed that with some successful years in weekly and two-weekly repertory theatres in England and Scotland. At first, because I was considered good looking and a ladies' man, they cast me mostly in romantic roles. In practice, however, I found I did best when I played the part of a cad or a ne'er-do-well—or even a buffoon. I enjoyed my most outstanding success in the role of Charles Stanton, the cheat and suave seducer in J. B. Priestley's 'Dangerous Corner.'

Later I restored a little of my faith in the better side of my character by playing in a romantic role at the Richmond Theater in London—a special performance for Queen Elizabeth's grandmother, Queen Mary. We played to a packed house—a wonderful mixture of members of London's high society and of ordinary working people. The play, 'Romance,' one of Queen Mary's favorites, had been selected at her request. It seemed to have pleased everyone, for at the final curtain we were given a standing ovation. Looking up at Queen Mary's box from my position in the curtain call lineup, I could see that she was applauding, too.

After the curtain had come down for the last time, that truly regal lady let it be known that she wished to meet the whole cast, and one at a time, we were escorted to her box. Before entering, we were given brief instructions on how best to conduct ourselves. If she offered her gloved hand, one would not shake it. One would place one's own hand under hers to raise it slightly, while bending as if to raise it to one's lips. One wouldn't quite get that far, one's lips would not actually touch her hand—it would simply be a symbolic gesture.

The ladies of the cast were advised that they would gently take her hand if offered, and simply curtsy. One was asked to remember that if the Queen engaged one in conversation, one should avoid prolonging it. At eighty-five years of age, long discussions could tire her. Better to answer whatever specific question she might ask, but resist any temptation to enlarge on it, and simply refer to her as 'Ma-am,' rather than 'Your Majesty.'

As we were to be presented to Queen Mary in alphabetical order, my turn came about half way through the list. When at last I stepped inside the red velvet drapes hanging at the entrance to her box, I found myself truly awed by her tall, statuesque appearance. A champagne-colored hat in the form of a silken turban accentuated her height.

Despite her most imposing presence, she was quick to put me at ease. She extended her hand as I had been advised that she might, and I bowed and lifted it a little in the manner I'd been instructed. Without waiting for me to speak, she began commenting on my performance in the play. I was so preoccupied with my concern to behave appropriately and avoid falling over my own feet that I didn't register exactly what she said. But I do know that in her rich and incisive voice, she was telling me how much she'd enjoyed the play—and specifically my part in it. She made me feel that I had done a wonderful job of acting, though in fact my part had been quite small.

'Thank you very much, ma-am,' I said. Then with a final bow, I backed carefully away from her august presence, and eased myself through the thick velvet drapes into the friendly embrace of the shadows beyond. A day to remember.

After that, I worked in small parts in motion pictures, and even took over a role for Robert Taylor for two full months when he was making the film 'Conspirator.' He was called back to Hollywood quite suddenly. A conflicting schedule left him with insufficient time to do anything except the close-ups and a few of the medium shots for his present film. To cope with that situation, the casting director called me in to the Elstree Studios to check out my profile against Taylor's. They made us stand back-to-back to compare our builds and height. When they were satisfied with that, they set to work with the make-up, and in the end only his co-star, Elizabeth Taylor, could tell us apart. Maybe that wasn't too surprising since the rest of the cast was mostly British and they hadn't met Robert Taylor before either.

After Taylor's departure I did everything else: the long shots, most of the medium shots, and even some of the near close-ups that he'd simply not had time for, so a good deal of the time, when viewers think they are watching Robert Taylor on the screen, they are actually watching me.

In the course of that exciting time, I almost got myself drowned in the duck-shooting sequence. We were out there, walking the 'Flats'—the vast stretches of sea-level flat land and mud banks on the East-Anglian coast, an area of the Fen district near the Wash, ideal for duck-shooting forays. One afternoon near sundown, when the camera sequence had been completed and the crew had left, I stayed behind with two other actors. We thought we might do a little private duck shooting ourselves. We became so engrossed with this that we didn't notice the onset of twilight, nor did we notice the increasing depth of the water we were wading through as the tide steadily advanced preparatory to submerging the entire area. Then one of our trio did notice.

"Hey, which way do we have to go to get out of here?" he called.

We looked around, a full 360 degrees. The gentle rise of the shoreline could no longer be seen. Whichever direction we looked we could see only water, with long ridges of mud banks projecting here and there above the surface. In the distance, we could see one or two lights ahead of us, and one or two behind. We couldn't tell whether they were on shore or whether their light came from ships or lighthouses.

In the end we simply took a vote on which direction to proceed. We walked for what seemed a very long time, with the depth of the water lapping at our shins hardly changing. From this we concluded that we must be walking more or less parallel to the shore, but approaching it at a shallow angle, just sufficient to offset the effect of the rising tide. By mid evening we discovered that our guesswork had been fairly accurate. We came ashore, wet and weary, some two miles from the point on the coastline where we'd set out that morning.

With our feet on dry land again, we talked of our experience of that day as if it had been a great adventure, but I reminded myself that with a wife and child to think about, I had better get more life insurance before getting involved in that sort of activity again. A couple of weeks later, still playing Taylor's part, I came close to piling up an expensive sports car in the Welsh mountains, so that by the time the shooting had run its course I was congratulating myself on having survived the whole adventure without injury.

Another part of me was facing the fact that I still didn't really care whether I lived or died.

With the tumult and the excitement over, I now had more time on my hands than I would have wished, and even before I'd left the Welsh mountains behind me, my nightmares had returned. I dreamed about the four of us being flung out of the Wolseley Hornet onto the damp grass. Then we all got to our feet and found that we were at the Rialto Casino, dancing. Verna's blood-covered eye was dripping profusely, staining her ice blue gown and making shiny red pools on the floor as we danced the tango. We went on like that with the pools of blood getting larger until the music of the dance band gradually changed to the insistent clanging of an ambulance bell. The clamor got louder and louder until I awoke gasping and trembling to the peace and quiet of our mountain hotel.

A couple of nights later I dreamed of Verna riding past me on her bicycle. I ran after her, never getting any closer. I fell in the middle of the road totally exhausted. A motor cyclist ran over me and I felt the wheels crush my chest, breaking my ribs. I could still hear them cracking as I awoke startled and bathed in sweat, yelling Verna's name. I pounded the bed with clenched fists, choking with anger and despair as I raged and ranted. I went on yelling, "Damn you Verna, Damn you to Hell. I hate you, I hate you!" Full wakefulness returned as I said the words.

"Oh my god, what am I saying? That's not true. I love you and I need you!"

"Goddamit, why won't you let me get on with my life!"

By this time, the whole film industry had fallen into a slump so that even the stars were having a difficult time finding work. Time to take stock of my situation and responsibilities. I had at any rate had my fling at what I really wanted to do and, I told myself, I could always return to the stage and motion pictures when more promising times would return.

TWENTY THREE

London 1952—1955

Relaxing in the train one day on my way home from the West End, an advertisement in the 'Help Wanted' section of the Daily Telegraph caught my eye. It was for someone to sell mobile radio-telephone equipment, and the advertiser was a company called Imhof Limited whose showrooms were at the north end of Tottenham Court Road.

I could sell mobile radio I told myself, and although, apart from the kind we used in airplanes, I didn't know much about it, I could certainly learn. Besides, I had a pretty good electrical and radio engineering background and that was bound to come in handy.

Without further hesitation I applied for the job and hoped I would have time to bone up on the subject in time for whatever interviews I might be invited to. I sat with pencil and paper, sorting out what I knew and what I didn't. I did know the difference between the methods used to carry sound waves on the backs of radio waves, from the sending aerial to the receiving aerial. The popular choices were frequency modulation and amplitude modulation and I knew the operating capabilities for which each of these techniques was best known. Basically, amplitude modulation (AM) had the better range but the frequency method (FM) was freer from static and other electrical noise. A few days later, a formal invitation for me to attend a 'preliminary' interview, arrived in the morning mail.

When I turned up for the interview, the owner, Godfrey Imhof, conducting the meeting, seemed satisfied with my general demeanor and the way I went about answering his questions. He explained, however, that the selection of a suitable candidate for the job would be made, not by him, but by executives from Pye Telecommunications Limited, who manufactured the equipment for which Imhofs held the London and Home Counties distributorship. He warned me that the differences in the types of modulation used in mobile radio communication were the primary factors that distinguished one brand of equipment from another, and that I should bear this in mind if I were to be invited to an interview with the Pye executives. I learned that the interviewers would be John Stanley, Vice President and son of the Chairman of the Pye Company, and Harry Woolgar, Director of Sales. They would certainly quiz me on this subject and I had better be sensitive to the fact that the Pye equipment was 'amplitude' modulated. I should beware of overstating its shortcomings.

A week or so later, Harry Woolgar, a seasoned and world-wise sales executive, is leaning against the mahogany liquor cabinet in Godfrey Imhof's office. Godfrey, with the air of the impartial observer, sits comfortably behind his desk. The much-discussed interview is in progress and John Stanley is running the show. He is pacing slowly back and forth on the Persian rug. A lock of straight blond hair hangs over his young and intense face. He is studying the intricate patterns on the rug as he asks:

"Mr. Layton—Howard isn't it—may I call you Howard? How would you describe amplitude modulation as applied to broadcasting?"

"It carries the program material or sound waves by varying the amplitude of the carrier radio wave," I reply. "And in public broadcasting, it's able to travel over long distances and cover large geographical areas." I glance at John Stanley to see whether I can get some hint of his reaction to my answer, but he continues pacing, his eyes on the carpet.

"How does it do that?"

"Do what?"

"Go long distances."

"Oh, by bouncing off buildings and ionized layers in the upper atmosphere. That way the radio waves can hop, skip and jump over large distances—sometimes all over the world—before they are dissipated."

"And how would you describe frequency modulation?"

"Frequency modulation continually adjusts the frequency of the carrier radio wave to convey the program material, instead of changing its amplitude. The amplitude stays constant."

Still no reaction from John Stanley. His pacing is beginning to unnerve me.

"What would you say is the chief feature of frequency modulation?" he says to the carpet.

I give him the answer I had rehearsed in front of the mirror the night before.

"Frequency modulation behaves a bit more like a beam of light. That is, it's substantially a line-of-sight method. The waves can travel good distances but they don't bounce off buildings or atmospheric layers very well. They tend to get absorbed, or simply go right through the atmospheric layers, so their range of operation is typically limited to between ten and twenty miles depending on how high the base-station antenna is located above the surrounding terrain."

John Stanley looks up from the carpet for the first time. "Hmm," he says with his intense gaze fixed on the office window, "And does frequency modulation have any special advantages to make up for its more limited range?"

Better watch it now. Safer to keep my answers fairly objective for the sake of credibility.

"What FM lacks in operating range it makes up for in its freedom from background noise and static," I reply. I am sweating now.

"Which do you think is the better method for mobile radio equipment?" The question is fired at me almost as an accusation. I throw caution to the winds.

"Depends on who is doing the selling," I shoot back.

A pause. Godfrey Imhof's eyes twinkle. He looks first at John Stanley, then at Harry Woolgar. "Any more questions gentlemen?" he asks.

For the first time in the interview, John Stanley looks directly at me.

"As soon as you've settled in, we'll want to see you for an in-depth briefing on the product line."

It was over. John Stanley and Harry Woolgar departed for Cambridge and it was up to me now to get on with the job and see whether I would be able to make the switch from frustrated thespian to applications engineer without falling on my face. But I was by no means alone. My partner in the office, 'Tup' Theakston, a veteran technical salesman himself, was already deeply involved in making the rounds of the taxicab companies and learning how to drink as they could drink—vodka and tomato juice by the tumbler. As far as I knew, Tup had missed out on the departmental management position because of his limited technical training. Even so, his ability to erect aerial masts was very impressive, and he was an effective salesman.

Then there was Helen Barr, slim, attractive, efficient secretary, whose organizing abilities, I soon discovered, were responsible for much of our successful sales promotion work. Our base transmitter dispatcher, Bobbie Bowery, and red-headed Vera, who worked on proposals, made up the rest of the crew. It was a congenial and productive team, and little by little with dogged perseverance, we began to develop our share of the mobile radio market. We held informative lectures at the headquarters of various prospective customers and began to foster a broader awareness of the practical value of the mobile radiotelephone.

My first real triumph concerned an opportunity to equip more than sixty South-London taxicabs with radio-telephones. I was invited to the fleet's headquarters for final negotiations and, if possible, to collect an order and a down-payment check. In the course of my presentation to the whole group a month previously, I had learned that there were special rites of passage that one had to observe to 'qualify' as a vendor to this particular company, and one's success would depend quite heavily on one's compliance with those rites. I was not quite sure what to expect when I drove up to the parking area at the front of the Waterloo building but whatever it was, I told myself, I was up to it.

The 'office' with its cobblestone-paved floor and high glass ceilings was actually a courtyard in front of the main building. It was like a miniature railroad station, but the chief, Fred Cobb, quickly made me feel at home. I found him sitting at the end of a large wooden table with his great bulk flowing over the arms of a high-backed basket chair. Waving at me with a tankard in his hand, and freely spilling an alcoholic brew of some sort over the table, he indicated that I should be seated next to him and that I should relax. Then he placed a glass beer tankard in front of me.

Instead of producing a bottle of good English Ale, however, a bottle of Plymouth Gin appeared as if from nowhere and my host proceeded to fill my tankard. He stopped at about the one-third mark, then, mistaking my dumbstruck silence and my open-mouthed stare as signs of approval, he continued to pour. I found my voice a bit later than the half-full moment and asked if I might have a little tonic water. He didn't have any of that, but instead brought forth a container of Noilly Prat vermouth and sloshed a generous helping into my tankard.

There were no negotiations. After ensuring that I was making some progress with my drink, Fred heaved himself up out of his chair, picked up some documents from the table beside him, and ambled toward the two large doors leading to the main building. At the door, he turned. "The men liked your presentation last month," he said. Then he disappeared into the main building, leaving me to contemplate my tankard of gin.

I was tempted to go after him—to ask about the status of the order—but something told me that that would be the wrong thing to do. I somehow knew that to conclude our negotiations in the desired manner, I was expected to finish my drink. I pondered my options. I did my best to calculate the amount of gin I had to consume. A pint-sized tankard holds a pint. That's sixteen ounces. At two-thirds full, that would amount to between ten and twelve ounces of liquor. Five or six two-ounce shots! Even the thought of it churned my stomach. Surreptitiously I glanced around trying to locate a drain or waste container where I could dump the contents of the tankard, but there was nothing to be seen. Besides, I had an uneasy feeling that I was being watched through one of the many front windows of the main building.

Again I considered barging through the double doors and tackling Fred about the order, and again some sixth sense told me that that would be a mistake. It was becoming increasingly clear to me that there was not going to be a way out. I would have to drink the stuff.

In the course of my wartime service with the RAF there had been occasions when a few double gins would not have fazed me. But that was many years ago and I was totally out of practice. Nowadays, a couple of glasses of wine were my usual quota and even that much alcohol was not entirely without its after-effects the following morning. I didn't know exactly how this present binge would affect me, but I decided that it would be best to prepare for the worst. I opened my briefcase to find something to write on, and as I was taking out my notebook, I saw the sandwich that I'd bought for lunch the day before and hadn't had occasion to need. It was a valuable find. Some food in my stomach would help to absorb the alcohol. I was thankful for small mercies. I pulled the sandwich out of my case and set it on the table beside me. I wrote a couple of notes, stuffed them into my jacket pocket and put the notebook back in my briefcase. Then I began to eat and drink.

Believing that nothing could be gained by protracting the process, I took gulps of my drink and bites of my sandwich alternately and fairly continuously. It was shortly after I'd consumed the last bite of the sandwich and reduced the contents of my tankard to about the quarter level that my head began to throb and my vision began to blur. The world began to turn in front of my eyes. I seemed to be on the merry-go-round at the Coventry Fairgrounds, finding it difficult to stay on my horse. If I concentrated really hard, I could focus my eyes just for a moment or two, then I would lose it and the world would spin again. Something told me that I had better not waste time. I made a grab for the tankard, felt its rim bang on my teeth as I swung it up to my mouth a little too energetically, and was vaguely aware of some trickling over my chin as I proceeded to drain it.

The timing seemed too precise to be coincidental. I had no sooner plonked the empty tankard back on the table, than Fred Cobb's bulk appeared in the double doorway. He ambled over to where I was sitting and stuffed some papers into my hand.

"Sorry it took so long," he said. "I think you'll find that in order."

I looked down with the feeling that the hand that was holding the papers didn't belong to me. I did my best to focus on the wording. By concentrating as hard as I could, I managed to ascertain that I was holding a purchase order and a check in my hand. I looked up and opened my mouth to thank my benefactor, but he was already disappearing through the double doors. I wasn't about to make any attempt to follow him. Difficult enough to make my way to the entrance of the courtyard without alerting any prying eyes to my precarious condition. I fumbled with my briefcase, stuffed the papers in, and by a prodigious effort of will, hauled myself up to a standing position.

Proceeding in what I hoped was a substantially straight line I made my way carefully to the entrance and turned the corner into the street. As my head began to throb in earnest and my vision became even more blurred, I knew I was running out of time to complete my plan. I passed my car, parked against the curb not far from the gates I had just come through, and made my way to the end of the street. There, I turned the corner and, leaning against a lamppost for support, I hailed a taxi.

Once inside the cab, I told the driver that I wasn't feeling well and that I would like to get to a public phone before going on to Imhof's Showrooms. We found a phone-booth within a minute or two but when I attempted to get out of the cab to make my call I found it quite beyond my capabilities. I fumbled for the two pieces of notepaper in my pocket, extracted some generous fare money from my wallet, and gave the papers and the money to the driver.

"Please make the call for me," I said, "and read the message to Godfrey Imhof." Then I passed out.

When I opened my eyes again, I was lying on the couch in Goff Imhof's office. Evidently the taxi driver and Goff had done well by me. As I learned later, the driver had dutifully called Goff, and had then driven to the Imhof showrooms and parked at the back door in Hanway Street where Goff was waiting to meet him. Goff, with the driver's help, had then smuggled me up in the rear elevator to his office where I would have a chance to recover from the worst effects of my overindulgence. Two cups of strong black coffee served to bring me back to some semblance of wakefulness. As I came to, I was greeted by the sight of Goff grinning at me broadly from behind his desk. As soon as I felt able to move, I reached for my briefcase and fumbled around for the hard-won purchase order and check. When I found them I handed them to Goff.

"I hope there are easier ways to get orders," I said. Then I fell back again into a deep and blissful slumber.

Success followed success and I became so involved with the daily challenges of the job that my determination to return to acting in a few months, steadily weakened.

The months turned into years, and at some point along the way I acknowledged to myself that the point-of-no-return had already slipped away. Yet I was still very restless, and I still could not get Verna out of my mind. I needed to find something more completely absorbing, something that would give me a chance to forget, and I just wasn't having any success in that quest. Besides, fascinating as mobile radio might be I could not see myself making a career of it, and in any case I didn't feel I was making enough money. Even after my crowning achievement in wresting the prestigious Automobile Association account away from Marconi, I was still finding it difficult to support my wife and child in the pretty little piece of suburbia that was our home.

Twelve Aston Avenue in Kenton, the attractive semi-detached where Laura and I now lived was all that we needed, but its upkeep accounted for a larger proportion of my income than we'd originally expected. In addition, Laura had felt it essential that we send Peta Pam to boarding school to broaden her horizons and her academic prospects, and this added expense strained our financial resources to the limit.

In the end we decided that we'd have a better chance of balancing our budget if we abandoned the tranquility of outer suburbia and moved to a flat closer to my place of work. We put our house on the market fully furnished and went flat-hunting closer to town.

St. John's Wood in northwest London is a lively and attractive community, well within the compass of the London Underground railway commuting network and boasting its own underground station. It was there that in the course of one of our Sunday afternoon prospecting tours, we stumbled upon a new block of flats in which three or four units were still available.

Kingsmill, a small but well-appointed apartment building, encompassed about forty flats in all. The spacious layout of the flats suited us well, and the location, less than five minutes walk from the Underground, could hardly have been more convenient. We found an agency office right on the ground floor of the building and were fortunate enough to get a tour of the available apartments on our first visit. Number fifteen on the second floor appeared to offer the space and layout we were looking for. A large living room with plenty of windows faced southeast, and a sizable bedroom with an adjacent bathroom and kitchen and dining area, were all directly reachable from the entrance hall.

We wanted to get an idea of what the place would look like when furnished, so we asked the agent whether she knew of a furnished unit with a similar layout that we could look at, preferably one with Danish-modern furnishings. Yes, she knew of such a unit. A Swedish couple on the ground floor had a flat with the same layout and the agent was sure they'd be glad to show it to us. She picked up the telephone, found the couple in, and got us invited downstairs. By the end of the afternoon we'd signed up. Laura was ecstatic. All our present furniture would go with the house and she would have the immense pleasure of furnishing the flat from scratch.

But bricks and mortar do not a home make, and soon after we'd settled into our new quarters I realized that very little of my own restlessness had subsided with the relocation. It was Saturday morning. The September sun cast faint window-frame shadows across the mushroom-toned wall-to-wall carpet, leaving the rest of the living room almost completely gray. A subdued setting, just right for brooding. Laura had already gone out shopping to Bowman's. When we had first agreed on the desired color and pattern for the settee we'd bought, Laura had had difficulty committing herself to the actual shade. When Bowman's delivered and installed it in our flat, she was quite sure they'd made a mistake. It couldn't be the shade she'd ordered, she said, and it just didn't go with the carpet or the Sapele mahogany-and-rosewood sideboard. They would just have to change it, and Laura had gone off to see about that.

Alone in the flat I began to review the patchwork quilt that was my life, and I thought about the events of recent years since my resignation from the service. Stage and film work had been exciting and enjoyable. I had performed before Queen Mary and had actually shaken hands with her. I had filled in for Robert Taylor for a couple of months when he found he couldn't do two movies at the same time. In the process I had come close to drowning myself in the Wash in East Anglia and narrowly escaped piling up an expensive sports car as I raced around the mountain roads of north Wales. Oh yes, it had been exciting enough, but it had got me precisely nowhere.

Perhaps if I'd been single and fancy-free I might have put up with the slings and arrows of that roller-coaster existence long enough to establish myself, but I had not had that luxury. One needed to start young in the acting business, and at twenty nine, my first agent had complained that I'd left it rather late. I had reminded her that there'd been a war on, but her response had not been sympathetic. "You should have got out at the end of the war instead of signing on again," she said. "I guess you just couldn't make up your mind what you wanted to do with your life." And of course she had been right. The war had interrupted my career and left me, like so many others, unsettled, and in a way, lost.

The switch to sales engineering and my job at Imhof's had probably been a good move in the circumstances. The long-term possibilities and the attainable heights in the business world were perhaps not as lofty or appealing as a career in stage and film work might have been, but the course would be less precarious and more financially rewarding on the way up. Yes, for a married man with responsibilities, it had been a move in the right direction. Not by any means a final move, but probably the right one. When Laura returned and told me of her successful discussions with Bowmans, I was in a more cheerful mood.

The Imhof RadioTelephone division continued to prosper. Aside from expanding the radio-telephone facilities of the Automobile Association and a multitude of police, fire, ambulance and taxicab services, we introduced this new communications tool to a growing number of London area businesses. Based upon our projections and estimates of the potential market for the product, we were formulating plans for a considerable expansion in general.

Things were going well—too well. Pye Telecommunications, the manufacturer of the equipment we were selling, decided that we were making too much money. They terminated the Imhof distributorship and took over the territory themselves. Goff, the accomplished businessman, managed to negotiate a handsome compensation for the loss of his Pye distributorship, but for me there was no other activity in the company that would be right for my kind of qualifications. I was a trained radio and electrical engineer and the other departments of Imhof's were strictly retail. They did not require my sort of background and would not make optimum use of it.

Goff thought otherwise. He offered me the management of his company's new high-fidelity department. He assured me that the task of growing that department to the size he intended for it, eventually eclipsing all other such outlets in London, would be fulfilling and financially rewarding for me. I was by no means convinced, but I listened attentively to the details of his offer. Sensing my doubts, he rounded off his presentation with a statement which, although proffered with the best of intentions and good humor, filled me with dismay. "Howard," he quipped, "so long as you don't steal the petty cash, you have a job here for life."

At Imhof's for life? Spend the rest of my days selling high-fidelity equipment to finicky, nit-picking retail consumers across London, when there was a big exciting world out there to be explored; use all those years of engineering training to sell the merits of a Wharfdale speaker or a Leak amplifier to temperamental music buffs or tone-deaf dentists while the world out there was overflowing with opportunities to market sophisticated machinery and instrumentation to industries all over the country, or even the whole wide world?

If Goff had just offered me the job instead of making it seem like a life sentence, it might have been different. Viewed as an interim occupation, to work at diligently until something more in line with my background could be found, it could be seen as a kind and generous offer. It was not too much to expect that a person suddenly losing the job of his or her choosing would be glad of any reasonable means of filling in, until suitable replacement employment could be found. But Goff had not put it that way. In his concern to assure me of his high opinion of my capabilities and of his desire that I continue as an Imhof employee, he'd scared me into the realization that I would have to leave—and soon.

I thanked Goff for his offer and for his faith in me. Then I told him of my decision to leave. He was visibly disappointed but he understood. He gave me the job anyway, and said that whenever I needed time off to attend a job interview I should just fit it into my work schedule and make sure that another member of the staff was suitably briefed to cover my absence. His generosity paid off, for almost a year elapsed before I closed my office door at Imhof's for the last time.

I went job hunting during the weekdays and took Laura sight-seeing at the weekends. We visited St. Paul's cathedral and the Tower of London. We spent an afternoon at Madame Tussauds and another at Westminster Abbey. All were places I'd visited with Verna in earlier years, and I had chosen them in my desperate and foolish attempts to relive the past, and to recall some of the wondrous days and evenings I had shared with Verna in those long ago times. Sometimes, after we returned from these outings, I would excuse myself and take an evening walk in the nearby park.

"I won't be long, Laura. I'll sleep better with a bit of fresh air before bed-time."

I walked and walked in a sort of trance, talking to Verna, apologizing for the way I'd treated her and begging her to let me get on with my life. Then moments later, I'd be chiding myself for being so spineless. Perversely, I found myself hoping that Verna was suffering as much as I. I made my way past Lord's cricket grounds and St. John's Wood underground station, wondering whether the ghost of all that I had so mindlessly destroyed all those years ago, would ever cease to haunt me.

It was not until a chance comment by a business friend opened up an opportunity for me to start a truly new life, free of constant reminders of my past and the pain of my loss, that I knew where my future lay. My business friend, Commander Victor Weake, also wrestling with his own transition to post-war life in his homeland, had met a certain John Ould while playing golf. John had mentioned that he was using a legacy from his deceased father to enter the international business arena. He had already opened an office in Berkeley square for himself and a secretary, and was looking for a partner for his enterprise.

Victor, familiar with my background and aware of my quest for a better future than a life at Imhof's could provide, had mentioned my name to John. He had made it clear that I was not in a position to make any kind of financial contribution, but that my engineering and sales background would more than make up for that constraint.

Victor arranged an introduction, and a few days later John and I were relaxing together at his club, sipping our coffee after a satisfying lunch of lentil soup, pork pie and salad. John leaned back in his chair and fixed me with a steady gaze. "I am a concert pianist," he said. He noted my surprise and paused for a moment to give me time to digest that information. Then he added, "But I have long felt that I'm not temperamentally suited for the life of a professional pianist and that I would feel more at home in the business world, preferably import-export." I couldn't understand why he would wish to give up such a fulfilling occupation just to switch to a career in business, but then, I reflected, while my reasons had been different, I'd done just about the same thing myself a few years previously. I made no comment, so he continued:

"Last year I inherited a goodly sum of money from my father and that windfall has given me the opportunity to make the switch to something I'd prefer to do."

"But why import-export?" I asked.

"Because it seemed to me a stimulating type of activity without requiring much in the way of a specialized education," John replied. "Also, I know the United States reasonably well, especially the East Coast, so I thought that would be a good place to start. My present objective is to open an office in New York as soon as practicable." Then he smiled a sort of kindly hurt smile and added, "I have a girl over there, too, so an office in New York would give me more opportunity to visit her and persuade her to marry me."

It all sounded very exciting and I began to get enthusiastic about the idea of joining him. But if John was planning to open a New York office, he would probably expect me to handle the home base at Berkeley Square and that didn't seem to be in line with my own objectives. I thought I had better explore that further.

"John, what exactly is your interest in me?" I asked.

"Well, from what I've learned, you have a strong technical background, so I thought we could work with products compatible with that background and experience."

I was flattered by the thought that he was considering shaping his enterprise around my particular expertise, but I could also see the drawbacks as well as the advantages. If we were able to secure export agencies with some reliable British manufacturers, technical expertise would be required to sell them in the USA, so John would need to get some technical training himself, and that would take time.

Still, to get the ball rolling while he set about educating himself in the required technology, he could, of course, take me with him to New York. That course of action would suit me very well. I decided to pursue this avenue.

"John, to sell electrical and electronic products you would need to acquire enough technical knowledge to be able to thoroughly understand their capabilities and sales features. That would take some time and if you don't mind my asking, I'm wondering how you'd deal with that and how you'd plan to get some sales going in the interim."

John looked at me, not quite comprehending. Then he laughed, "No, no," he said.

"You misunderstand me. I don't plan to do the selling. That would be your job. I have it in mind that I shall run the London office and you will take care of the New York end."

It took me a minute or two to absorb that pronouncement.

"Do you have an office there yet—a base of operations?" I asked.

"No, nothing. I would leave it to you to set that up. I'd give you a budget of course, and you would work with that."

My stomach churned a bit. This was going to be something more of a challenge than I'd been aiming for. John Ould turned his kindly eyes directly upon me and smiled.

"Why don't you go home and discuss the idea with your wife? If you both decide that this kind of adventure appeals to you, we can meet again and make arrangements to get the show on the road."

"When would you want me to start if we came to an agreement?" I asked.

"Well, just as soon as you could cut loose from your present job." He paused.

"We should probably spend about three months fixing up some agencies, then I think it would be a good idea to get you over to the States as soon as possible."

I took my leave. Plenty to think about—both exhilarating and scary at the same time, but it would get me to foreign shores, and that's where I wanted to be, wasn't it? Better find out what Laura would have to say.

Back home in St. John's Wood, I immediately telephoned the Tourist Department of the American Embassy to update myself on the climate in the United States.

"How much sun do you have?" I asked the travel representative.

"Well, the sun is always shining *somewhere* in America. It's a big country. What part are you interested in?"

"Oh, yes, of course." I'd forgotten how big the United States really is. "Let's talk about the climate in the New York area."

By the time I put the phone down I'd discovered that New York enjoyed considerably more hours of sunshine per annum than any part of the British Isles.

With this encouraging information to hand I joined Laura at the dinner table and briefed her on my interview with John Ould.

We talked long into the night. To my surprise I found Laura quite taken with the idea of setting up in New York. She seemed confident that we would make a go of it, and quite fascinated with the idea of moving to another big city area. She did insist, however, that for the present, our nine-year-old daughter, Peta Pam, would remain at the boarding school in Lyminge, Kent, where she'd been enrolled the previous year. Laura's thought was that at holiday times we would simply arrange for her to fly to New York to join us.

By morning we'd made our decision and were already planning the sale of our flat, and on February 10th 1955, Laura and I, with all our worldly goods, boarded the SS United States, and set off on our journey to a new world and a new life.

For the second time in my life, as I stood at the rails at the stern of the ship and stared at the receding shores of the Liverpool docks, I could see Verna's smiling face through the rolling mists. I raised my two hands and cupped them around a lovely face that wasn't there, and I bade her a silent goodbye.

"Take care my darling," I called softly as the outline of her face receded again and merged with the shadows of the night. "Take care."

I stood there against the rails for a few minutes more, peering into the fathomless dark. A little girl whom I hadn't previously noticed, swung back and forth on the rails beside me. I felt her staring at my face.

"Why are you staring at me, young lady," I asked.

She thrust a hand into one of the pockets of her beige tweed coat and pulled out a wrinkled lace-edged handkerchief. She held it up and motioned me to take it.

"You can keep it," she said, "I've got another one." Her eyes glistened.

"Grown-ups aren't supposed to cry. It makes me want to cry, too."

I dabbed my eyes with her handkerchief and smiled down at her.

"Well then, we just won't do that any more."

I thanked her and walked back toward the stairway to our cabin, waving to her as I did so.

"See you later," I called.

As I made my way to join Laura, I vowed once more, this time silently, that from now on I would use all of my energy and resources to make a better life for her and for Peta Pam.

From this time forward, there would be no people or places, no friends or mutual acquaintances, no Midland-Red buses or bluebell-filled woods, no Kenilworth or Warwick Castles to remind me of those precious times I'd shared with Verna. No day trips to Westminster Abbey or St. Paul's; no semi-detached brick houses with their slate-tiled roofs and rose gardens out front, to bring her gaiety and wondrous smile to my mind; I would no longer come across fields of daffodils or thatch-roofed cottages and country pubs, so prevalent in the winding country lanes of England, to relive those precious outings we'd reveled in together. There would be no Rialto Casino or Leicester Palais de Dance, where the music of the orchestras of Henry Hall or Ambrose would bring Verna's graceful twirling form and clinging ice-blue gown into my reveries. Perhaps, somewhere in and among those deep canyons of commerce between the endless rows of skyscrapers in the great cities of America, we would find a new life together, Laura and I, and our little girl.

And perhaps, in time . . . I would find peace.

FINIS

Peta Pam who tipped the scales

AND LATER YET

My longing to fly stayed with me, and in 1973, at age fifty five, I learned to fly, eventually earning an instrument rating and a commercial license. By that time I had my own manufacturing business, so I bought a six-seat, high performance airplane, and used it for many years to visit and serve my customers. When I flew my Piper Saratoga for the last time, I had logged more than a thousand piloting hours.

Even today as I write, I still have my commercial pilot's license and current FAA medical certificate, so that if the mood strikes me, I can still go out to the local airfield, rent an airplane—and fly.

POSTSCRIPT

As things turned out, my attempts to make Laura happy while simultaneously trying to establish the business enterprise I'd founded, proved beyond my capabilities. Within a few years of our arrival in the New World, Laura's preferences for English traditions and more conservative ways of life persuaded her to leave me and return to the 'Old Country.' In 1961, we were divorced.

It was not until a happy turn of fate brought Nárcissza into my world that I learned the true meaning of unswerving loyalty and steadfastness, and found a new purpose in my life.

Nárcissza and I walked down the aisle together in 1962. In all, we raised six children. We started right off with Peta Pam and Peta Pam's sister Leslie. Then we added three children of our own, Christine, Alison and Paulette, and somewhere along the road, we adopted Nárcissza's nephew Antal when his parents were killed in an auto crash.

But that's another story and another book.

Some months after our engagement, Verna had accidentally dropped her elegant opal ring, and sometime later a fine crack appeared across the face of the opal itself. I do not know whether Verna continued to wear the ring after I went overseas, but I am superstitious about such things. At any rate, since that time, I have never bought an opal ring, or any other opal jewelry, for my wife, my daughters, or for anyone.

Verna eventually married, but the union was not a happy one, and it ended in an early separation. However, she was blessed with a lovely daughter, Rosemarie, who is now happily married to husband Martyn. They have two fine children of their own—Clare and Robert, and a granddaughter Rhian.

Verna passed away in 1965 as the result of a heart attack.

After the war, Elaine Stemmet was publicly honored for her tireless work in writing and sending parcels to the countless servicemen and women whom she had befriended during their short stays-over in Capetown, and had 'adopted' for the duration of the war. Elaine eventually visited each one of those who survived, myself included.

Squadron Leader James Maitland Pike, whose daring and skill made all the difference on that fateful day in 1941, retired from the Royal Air Force in 1969 with the rank of Air Commodore. When I attempted to reach him late in 1999 to ask for his own recollections of that memorable flight together, I learned that he had passed away a few months previously, leaving no relatives of record.

That enchanting spot in Capetown, where Johnny and I once dined so royally with Fred and Elaine Stemmet, has taken on different faces with different owners since the time of our visit in 1941. But perhaps, here and there, among others who traveled that magic route during those times, there will be one or two good souls who will read this account and say "Ah, yes, I was there once, and I remember that place with the deep blue sky and the forever crescent moon."

Several art-pieces adorn the walls of my studio in Connecticut, each of which I regard as a very special souvenir. Among them there's a young man fishing from a pier with a blood red sunset as his background. It was painted by a good friend who died a few years ago. Then there's a magical industrial-complex scene belching smoke that almost gets in my throat whenever I look at it. That's by an advertising artist who, in years gone by, created brochures for my family business.

And in the center of the end wall, there's a haunting scene of couples strolling arm–in-arm along a tree-lined boulevard in Paris. It is signed 'Gabri.'

And the Golden Hind—That labor of love which once embodied all my hopes and dreams? That noble relic of another time has found its final resting-place in the glass display case of a country dining room in Connecticut.

When Verna passed away, her family returned the ship to my brother Archie who in turn sent it on to me by ocean freight. The model ship was badly damaged in transit, and because of the broken dreams it symbolized, I chose not to repair it. The proud model, now a gaunt and darkened wreck, with splintered masts and tattered sails, speaks to me of glories past; of a time long gone that was full and rich; of a love that I destroyed.

REFERENCES

A FEW GOOD BOOKS ON THE DESERT WAR

ALAMEIN, by Jon Latimer. Harvard University Press, Cambridge, MA.

AN ARMY AT DAWN by Rick Atkinson. Owl Books, Henry Holt & Company, New York.

BLENHEIM SQUADRONS OF WORLD WAR TWO by Jon Lake. Osprey Publishing, Michelin House, 81 Fulham road, London SW3 6RB.

THE DESERT RATS by Major General C. L. Verney DSO, MVO GreenhillBooks, Lional Leventhal Ltd., Park House, 1 Russel Gardens, London NW11 9NN

DESERT WAR, by Alan Moorehead. Penguin Books, Penguin Putnam Inc.,
375 Hudson Street, New York, NY 10014 USA.

EIGHTH ARMY'S GREATEST VICTORIES by Adrian Stewart. LEO COOPER, Pen and Sword Books, Ltd. 47 Church Street, Barnsley, South Yorkshire, S70 2AS.

HIDDEN VICTORY, The Battle of Habbaniya, by Air Vice-Marshal A. G. Dudgeon, CBE, DFC. Tempus Publishing Ltd., The Mill, Brimscombe Port, Stroud, Gloucester, GL5 2QG UK

PAN AFRICA. Across the Sahara in 1941 with Pan Am, by Tom Culbert and Andy Dawson. Paladwr Press, 1906 Wilson Lane, Apt.101, McClean, VA 22102-1957

THE WINSTON SPECIALS by Archie Munro. Maritime Books, 2006

ORDER FORM

Fax orders: (203) 794-0209

Telephone orders: (203) 748-5624

E-mail orders: howardlayton@sbcglobal.net

Postal orders: THREE SPIRES PUBLISHING, P.O. Box 5267, Brookfield, CT 06804 USA

Please send the following book(s):

I understand that I may return any book for a full refund—for any reason, no questions asked.

Name: _____

Address:_____

City: _____State: _____ Zip: _____

Telephone: (   ) _____

Sales Tax:
Please add 6% for books shipped to Connecticut addresses.

Shipping:

$4 for the first book. $2 for each additional book.
Payment: ☐ Check Enclosed
☐ Bill me at the following address:

Wreckage of the Golden Hind model

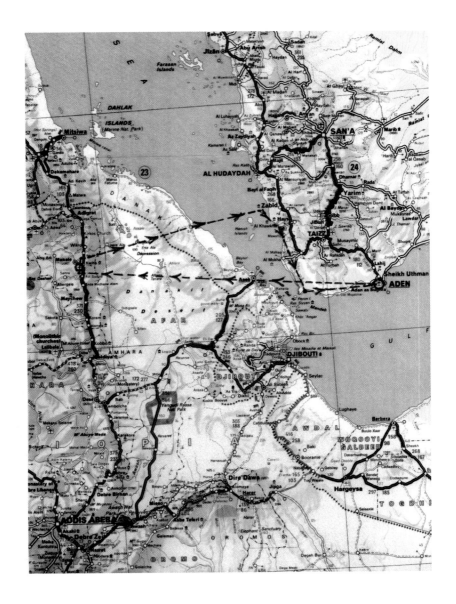

Route of Raid on Makale, Abbysinia
Feb 4, 1941
(Map 1)

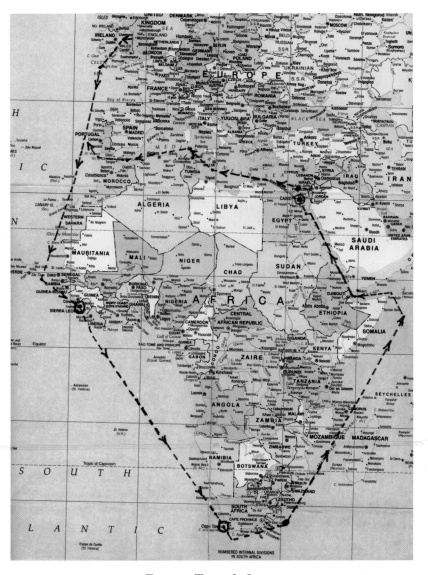

Routes Traveled
By The Author
1940 and 1945
(Map 2)

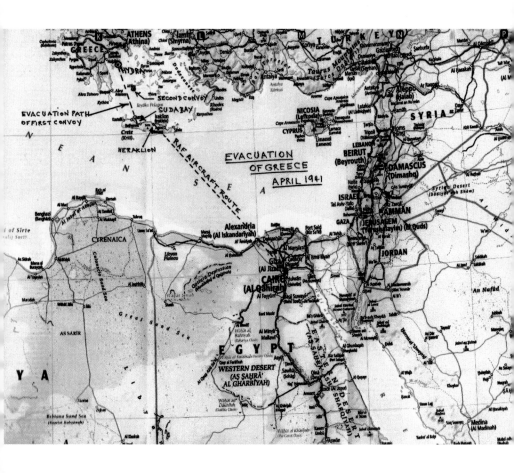

Escort Route of the Evacuation of Greece
April 1941
(Map 3)